BRAILLE LITERACY

A Functional Approach

DIANE P. WORMSLEY

Frances Mary D'Andrea, CONSULTING EDITOR

AFB PRESS
NEW YORK

Printed in the United States of America

Library of Congress Cataloging-in-Publication Data

Wormsley, Diane P., 1946–
    Braille literacy : a functional approach / Diane P. Wormsley.
        p.   cm.
    Includes bibliographical references and index.
    ISBN 0-89128-876-7
    1. Braille—Study and Teaching—United States.   2. Literacy—Study and teaching—United States.   3. Children, Blind—Education—United States.   I. Title.
    HV1672.W64   2003
    411—dc22   2003045117

All photographs by Diane P. Wormsley

Braille Literacy: A Functional Approach was made possible in part by generous support from Miss Marion I. Breen.

The American Foundation for the Blind—the organization to which Helen Keller devoted more than 40 years of her life—is a national nonprofit whose mission is to eliminate the inequities faced by the ten million Americans who are blind or visually impaired.

It is the policy of the American Foundation for the Blind to use in the first printing of its books acid-free paper that meet the ANSA Z39.48 Standard. The infinity symbol that appears above indicates that the paper in this printing meets that standard.

Dedicated to the Staff and Students
at Overbrook School for the Blind
without whom this book would
not have been possible.

Contents

Foreword

For many of us, helping people learn to read and write is one of the chief joys of the teaching profession. Reading books with children, writing stories together, and helping children make sense of the printed word is an experience of shared discovery and growth for both the student and the teacher. For teachers of adults, helping learners crack the code that has long eluded them or helping non-English-speaking learners to read and write in a new language gives deep satisfaction.

Teachers of students who are blind or visually impaired and rehabilitation teachers have the additional pleasure of instructing people to read and write in braille. The look of "ah ha!" on a learner's face as the patterns of bumps become words, sentences, and ideas is what keeps many teachers motivated and enthusiastic about their careers. Even with the advent of new and more sophisticated technology that "reads" aloud from a computer screen or enlarges images, there is wide recognition that braille is equal to print as a literacy medium—and is just as necessary.

Sometimes, though, we encounter a student who struggles to learn to read, and all our tried-and-true methods just don't seem to work. Approaches that are successful with other students, commercially available programs, or prepackaged materials just don't seem to do the trick. It can be as frustrating for teachers as it is for our students when reading and writing doesn't come easily, because we want learners to be successful and to become as literate as possible. We know the benefits that literacy can bring: Beyond academic and vocational success, literacy also brings an improved quality of life. We want reading to be enjoyable, and students for whom reading is difficult rarely find it enjoyable. These students need something different—an individual approach. It is for these students and their teachers and family members that this book was written.

In *Braille Literacy: A Functional Approach,* Diane Wormsley describes an approach to braille reading and writing instruction that taps into the learner's individual likes (and dislikes), specific needs, and individual goals. The approach is "functional" in that it starts from where the student is, and builds on personal experiences to introduce vocabulary that is meaningful to the learner. The approach works with adults who are learning braille for the first time as well as with children. This is not a "cookbook" approach, but it clearly describes steps in an approach that can be individualized and shaped around the student's life. The goal is to make braille functional for these learners by using a method that selects the most useful words for reading and writing *for that individual.*

Kliewer and Landis (1999) cite Burton Blatt, who said, "All people are educable. The orientation of those who would help [a person with disabilities] must be to find ways of teaching and bringing about growth—not to determine whether it is possible" (p. 98). The use of the approach described in this book may make it possible for individuals who have significant learning challenges to gain some proficiency in braille reading and writing, and bring about the growth that allows our students to reach their full potential.

Frances Mary D'Andrea
Director, National Literacy Center
American Foundation for the Blind

Braille, Reading, Literacy, and At-Risk Learners

What you bring to the reading process,
determines what you will take away.

—BECOMING A NATION OF READERS, 1985

B raille has been the primary reading medium for persons who are blind or severely visually impaired for well over 100 years, since Louis Braille perfected the braille code in 1834 (Hatlen, 2000). People may learn to use braille as a tool for literacy at any age, depending on their need for a medium other than print. Braille, like the letters of the printed alphabet it represents, is a personal, portable system for communication with oneself and others (see "What Is Braille?").

Traditional Teaching Approaches

Since the printed alphabet and braille are both symbol systems for reading and writing, approaches to braille instruction parallel those that exist for teaching print. Instructional programs and materials that are used for teaching print reading can often be used for teaching braille, with some modification (for example, students using texts containing illustrations and graphics will need these visual elements explained verbally or in writing). It is also important that children who are blind or visually impaired have well-developed concepts about their world. Concept development is easy when one can see. Developing concepts about a world that is too far away, too hot, too cold, too dangerous, too small to touch is difficult

WHAT IS BRAILLE?

Braille characters are formed from 63 various combinations of six dots arranged three high and two wide in a cell-like pattern. There are two primary forms of braille—uncontracted and contracted. Uncontracted braille, previously referred to as alphabetic or grade 1 braille, consists of the alphabet plus punctuation and "literary" numbers. (There is also a form of braille for mathematical and scientific notation, known as Nemeth Code, that uses different number signs, as well as music braille, an international code for music notation; and computer braille code, often taught to high school students and others involved in programming and technical aspects of working with computers.)

Contracted Braille

Standard braille, officially known as contracted braille, was previously called grade 2 braille, and consists of the alphabet, punctuation, plus various part- and whole-word contractions (such as specific signs for the letters *er,* or *tion*) and short forms (using just the letter *s* for *so,* etc.). This expands the number of basic symbols to be learned for reading literary material to over 180, in contrast to approximately 60–70 symbols in print. Since 1932, standard or contracted braille has been the approved code for reading and writing braille in the United States. It is generally assumed that being able to read and write contracted braille is the goal for anyone wishing to achieve formal braille literacy, since most books and magazines use this form of the code. However, in recent years, more materials are becoming available in uncontracted braille for both adults and for children.

Grade 3 Braille

In addition to standard braille, there is also a highly contracted form referred to as grade 3 braille, which is used mainly as a notetaking code for personal use or by students in college. While some training materials and a list of contractions that constitute grade 3 braille are available, grade 3 is seldom used for general reading materials. The rules for grade 3, with the list of contractions are contained in Rodenberg (1977). A complete set of the braille alphabet and contractions can be found on the Internet at the Braille Reference desk <http://www.brl.org/refdesk/indexes/>.

for children who are blind or visually impaired. With well-formed concepts and vocabulary that is based upon concrete meaningful experiences, children who are blind or visually impaired will have more to bring to the reading process, and thus will have more to learn from reading.

There are many ways to teach reading and writing (Duffy & Hoffman, 1999). Most balanced approaches draw from a continuum of activities, ranging from skills centered to meaning centered, based on the needs of the students. (See "Literacy Terminology" for definitions of these and other terms.) At various times, the individual skills that must be mastered in learning to read and write are emphasized. For example, a review of research in specific areas of reading identified four skill areas that can be beneficial to reading achievement: phonemic awareness, phonics, fluency, and comprehension strategies (National Reading Panel, 2000). Although skills are important, it is equally important that the meaning is derived from reading and conveyed through writing. With meaning-centered approaches, high-quality literature and the child's own language are the bases for the instruction, rather than basal readers, whose text has been contrived to achieve a certain reading level (Rex, Koenig, Wormsley, & Baker, 1994). Both the development of skills and the derivation of meaning from the text are important, and as the child engages in literacy activities, skills and meaning are both reinforced.

Most children who are blind and who have no additional impairments learn to read and write standard braille successfully. Like sighted children, some may respond better to specific approaches; for example, some children may learn better with an explicit rather than an implicit approach to the acquisition of phonics and other skills. Overall, with daily direct instruction from a trained teacher of students with visual impairments, and with modifications such as those described earlier, blind students learn to read and write very much like sighted students (Swenson, 1999; Wormsley & D'Andrea, 1997).

When Alternative Teaching Approaches Are Needed

Some children, however, are slow to learn to read braille no matter what approach is used. Several groups of individuals often have difficulties in

LITERACY TERMINOLOGY

The *meaning-centered approach* to teaching reading focuses on the reader's knowledge and experience. The emphasis is on deriving meaning from what is written (Rex, Koenig, Wormsley, & Baker, 1994).

The *skills-centered approach* focuses on decoding print symbols into words and emphasizes the component skills in reading (Rex, Koenig, Wormsley, & Baker, 1994).

The *literature-based approach* is a meaning-centered approach that utilizes interesting and challenging children's literature and focuses on meaning, interpretation, and enjoyment (Rex, Koenig, Wormsley, & Baker, 1994).

The *language experience approach* focuses on use of children's oral language and real-life experiences as the basis for creating personalized reading materials (Mason & Au, 1990).

The *balanced approach* is an interactive approach that selects from all of the various approaches according to the needs of the learner and the context of instruction. It is sometimes referred to as "eclectic" (Wormsley, 2000).

Phonemic awareness is the ability to break words into syllables or sounds and blend these parts together again (Swenson, 1999).

Phonics refers to the graphophonic system, or the association of a letter or group of letters with a corresponding sound (Swenson, 1999).

Fluency, sometimes referred to as "automaticity," is the ability to read a passage without stopping to decode or reread to understand its meaning (Wormsley, 2000).

Reading comprehension strategies are ways for students to improve and demonstrate comprehension by explicit and implicit means. "Explicit" means include retelling and including facts and details present in the stories. "Implicit" means include predicting outcomes, interpreting, inferring, drawing conclusions and making generalizations, and summarizing (Miller, 1995).

learning braille, particularly in learning standard contracted braille with its many rules. These at-risk learners include children with visual impairments who have additional or multiple impairments, including cognitive impairments, deaf-blindness, or physical limitations that inhibit their access to the environment. Other groups that tend to have difficulties with braille are older children or adults who may or may not have learned to read print, including those with limited English proficiency who are learning English as a second language. These are learners for whom the traditional approaches to teaching reading may not be successful.

In general, children with visual impairments have not seen models of reading and writing to the extent that sighted children have by the time they reach school, and so have had fewer experiences with written communication to assist them in acquiring beginning literacy skills. Children with additional disabilities are no different, but at-risk students have additional hurdles to overcome. Their limitations in cognitive development may include large gaps in concepts, including understanding of basic direction and location concepts, such as right, left, top, bottom, and so on. They often do not have sufficient vocabulary to take advantage of an entirely meaning-centered approach, so teachers often resort to teaching the alphabet and sounds in a rote manner. With a rote method, the children may succeed in reading a few letters of the alphabet, or even learn to write the entire alphabet (depending on their physical limitations), but often have difficulty actually reading and applying the rules of phonics and other skills. They often exhibit little comprehension or fluency.

At some point teachers may be tempted to give up on these children, declaring that the independent living or vocational skills that they must learn are more important than learning to read and write. In particular, children who are deaf-blind have severe communication needs that may be deemed so critical that formal literacy or "reading and writing" is not immediately included in the curriculum. Yet, it is the students who have the most difficulties who need more opportunities to participate in literacy activities, not fewer (Kliewer & Landis, 1999). It is important that these students see reading and writing in braille as a part of their lives—perhaps even more important than for children who are developing typically, because they cannot generalize from their experiences as readily.

These children can benefit from a functional approach that makes reading a more meaningful activity within their vocabulary and experiences, rather than simply teaching individual letters and trying to blend the letters into sounds. This approach can be integrated easily with the teaching of independent living, vocational, or communication skills, depending on a child's needs, which is the reason for calling this a functional approach. The literacy activities used in the functional approach actually serve to reinforce the learning of these functional life skills. The approach described in this book will provide teachers with a framework to use to integrate literacy instruction into the curriculum of their students who are having difficulty learning braille with more traditional teaching methods.

Older children and adults who are learning braille after previously reading print may also be identified as being at risk of not learning braille. These older children and adults may exhibit various levels of literacy in print and may be less motivated than younger children to learn to read braille. Those who have achieved a fairly high level of literacy and are accustomed to reading with fluency and speed may initially become discouraged and frustrated when learning braille. It takes time to develop speed and accuracy of character recognition in braille reading. They may decide that they can never reach a comfortable reading pace, and give up. Those who did not achieve a high level of literacy with print are essentially still learning to read and now having to do it with a different set of symbols. In addition, those who are learning English as a second language frequently have difficulty with a traditional approach. Any difficulty one might have learning braille is compounded when attempting to learn it using a language with which one is not familiar. For all these at-risk learners, a more functional approach can be the key to the beginning of successful braille literacy instruction.

A Functional Approach to Teaching Braille Literacy

A functional approach to braille literacy begins with the premise that students who have special difficulties learning to read and write braille are more successful if the words or letters being learned in the initial stages of braille reading have meaning or are functional for the learner. In this sense, the approach falls closer to the meaning-centered end of the continuum of traditional approaches. Although meaning-centered approaches are sometimes criticized due to their perceived lack of emphasis on phonics and other specific skills (Rayner, Foorman, Perfetti, Resetsky, & Seidenberg, 2002), approaches that are totally skills based—in which abstract letters are paired with sounds and then joined together to make words—do not always work well with at-risk learners who have visual impairments. These learners, who have had very little exposure to literacy, benefit from repeated, concrete, and meaningful experiences to understand basic concepts (Lowenfeld, 1973).

To understand the functional approach, one must understand how literacy develops. There are two generally agreed-on stages: emergent literacy and academic literacy. During the first stage, emergent literacy, learners become familiar with written language and develop concepts related to reading and writing. These concepts include how and for what purpose people read and write, as well as the tools they use. They learn concepts related to books and lines of print (or braille), such as top of page, bottom of page, turn the page, beginning of the line, end of the line, and so on. They develop experiences with written language at home and in the community that provide the basis for their later literacy learning. However, some students can remain in the emergent literacy stage for a much longer period of time than typically developing students. Some students do not truly catch on to braille reading and writing until they are middle school age—or even older.

The second stage of literacy (which can actually be broken down into several substages depending on whose theory is used) is "academic" or "basic" literacy. Academic literacy typically begins in kindergarten or first grade and extends through high school or beyond. During this stage, learners first learn to read and then use that capability to acquire more knowledge. Learners reach varying levels of sophistication within this stage and essentially can continue to progress throughout the life span.

During the acquisition of academic literacy, learners also acquire functional literacy skills. In general, functional literacy refers to the use of literacy in daily life for such basic tasks as making grocery lists, reading recipes, using automatic teller machines, paying bills, filling out job applications, reading instruction manuals for various appliances, and so on. (D'Andrea, 1997). Generally, learners' functional literacy skills correspond to their level of academic literacy. Some tasks—for example, filing income tax forms or reading computer software manuals—require a higher degree of academic literacy skills than do writing down and reading a grocery list or a telephone number. The use of the term *functional* in the functional approach to braille literacy suggests to some people only this latter aspect of functional literacy—using literacy for functional tasks. However, in this book, *functional* also refers to the vocabulary used in teaching reading. That is, the vocabulary used in a functional approach must be meaningful, as well as useful or functional, for these at-risk learners.

The functional approach draws upon a method of teaching reading that was used by Sylvia Ashton Warner and described in her book, *Teacher* (1963). Warner taught Maori children in New Zealand. Their cultural background was very different from that described in the basal readers that were standard fare for "infant" (primary) classrooms at the time. To help her students cross that cultural bridge, Warner always began teaching her Maori students to read by using "organic key words"—those words that elicited an emotional response in the children she taught. The strong emotion attached to the words the Maori students learned drew them into reading and made it real for them.

The functional braille literacy approach begins in the same manner as Warner's approach. Teachers select with the learner a key vocabulary from words that are within the learner's experience. The more emotionally attached the learner is to the words, the more motivation the learner has to read them. Teachers should respect the learner's choices of words. Warner found that sometimes the most motivating words were those that scared the students, such as *knife* or *fight,* because these words were part of their everyday experiences in the *pa,* or village, and were very emotionally based.

Unlike the Maori children, who were capable of selecting their own vocabulary, some at-risk learners have difficulty thinking of words. Teachers can help by suggesting the names of friends or family members, or action verbs that are exciting for the learner. Having intimate knowledge of what the learner likes is extremely important when selecting this vocabulary. The key words may or may not be related to functional life-skills tasks. These words are learned as whole units, although learners may initially use attributes such as length or tactilely distinct letters to recognize the words. The ability to recognize these whole words is gradually extended into a more skills-based approach by teaching letter recognition and phonics using the initial letters of the key vocabulary words (as they are mastered), or from tactilely distinct letters within the words. As opposed to teaching letters in an abstract order that has no meaning to the student, letters derive their meaningfulness from their identification with the already-known key vocabulary words. The key words then become functional or useful in expanding a learner's skills. Reading becomes meaningful and functional, to the best of the learner's abilities. This approach is similar to the "authentic literacy instruction" used in adult literacy (Purcell-Gates, Degener, Jacobson, & Soler, 2002).

The functional approach may also be extended to incorporate elements of the language experience approach, another meaning-centered approach, depending on the capabilities of the learner. The language experience approach focuses on the use of oral language and real-life experiences as the basis for creating personalized reading materials (Mason & Au, 1990). The steps in the language experience approach include (Leu & Kinzer, 1991)

- participating in an experience that will provide content for a story

- having learners describe the experience in their own words

- assisting them to create a story (usually as a group)

- writing that story on a chart (or, in the case of braille, on a braillewriter)

- helping students read what has been written.

The language experience approach has some intrinsic limitations, however, in that it can only introduce students to language that is already within their grasp. Some teachers may expand learners' vocabulary when writing stories by providing them with words for their experiences that are currently not within their vocabulary. But for the most part, using only a language experience approach limits students to reading only what they have written. This is not as serious a limitation for students who are not developing typically, since the goal is to have them eventually reading something that will be useful to them in their daily lives. Beginning with a functional approach for at-risk learners allows them to be successful with reading what is familiar to them, and provides a foundation for extending their skills into a quasi-academic literacy level, depending on the capabilities they demonstrate.

Who Should Read This Book?

Anyone who is interested in improving literacy instruction of braille readers should be able to find something helpful in this book. While it is designed primarily for teachers of visually impaired students and rehabilitation teachers who will be teaching braille reading and writing to the at-risk populations mentioned, it may also assist parents wishing to help their own children with reading and writing braille. Teachers who use more traditional approaches may find ideas to help certain students "over the hump" when they are having difficulties in reading. The approach may also be used initially in combination with a more traditional approach with any learner, including prekindergarten and kindergarten students, with or without disabilities, just as the language experience approach is often used in combination with other approaches.

Part 1 of this book provides the general guidelines for a functional braille literacy approach that can be followed with learners for whom a traditional approach is not appropriate or not successful. The twelve steps that make up the approach are discussed for both children and adults, and instances where steps may be used simultaneously with each other are outlined. In addition some forms for helping to individualize the approach are provided. Part 2 provides examples of how the approach can be modified for different types of at-risk learners through a number of case studies. While the case studies do not provide examples of how each of the twelve steps is utilized with every subject, the reader should receive enough information from the case studies to be able to reconstruct the approach with a similar learner.

Part 1

Creating an Individualized Functional Braille Literacy Program

This section provides the reader with general steps in creating an individualized functional braille literacy program. As mentioned previously, the learner for whom a functional literacy approach is considered is one who is generally unable to learn to read through traditional methods and may never achieve basic or academic literacy skills. Part 2 will provide examples of how the program can be adapted for individuals in the various populations discussed in the introduction. Even when learners appear to be similar, the individualized program created for one learner may not work for another. Indeed, individualization—using what is meaningful to the learner as the focus for reading and writing—is the key to the functional approach. Although the components or steps of a functional approach may look similar to the components of a traditional approach, there are two distinct differences in the functional approach: (1) the individualized vocabulary with which the teacher and student begin, and (2) how the teacher incorporates all of the other components into a personalized approach for students who are not "typical" learners.

There are several steps to take in setting up a functional literacy program for a learner (see sidebar). These steps follow a sequence and are discussed separately in the sections that follow. However, once teachers become familiar with the approach, they will most likely perform many

STEPS IN SETTING UP A FUNCTIONAL BRAILLE LITERACY PROGRAM

1. Determine whether braille will be the literacy medium, and which form of braille to use.

2. Create a braille-rich environment.

3. Select the individualized reading and writing vocabulary.

4. Create word boxes and flash cards and teach the first key words.

5. Teach tactile perception and letter-recognition skills through proper hand and finger usage in tracking activities.

6. Assess phonemic awareness.

7. Teach phonemic awareness.

8. Develop writing skills: mechanics and process.

9. Create functional uses for reading and writing.

10. Create stories.

11. Keep detailed records and use diagnostic teaching.

12. Watch for when to move to a more traditional academic approach.

of the steps simultaneously. For example, although they are presented separately for clarity, reading and writing skills need to be developed simultaneously. Several of the steps, such as creating a braille-rich environment and record keeping, will be ongoing throughout the learner's program. The functional braille literacy program works for adults as well as for children. However, many of the steps involve teaching skills that young children need to learn but adults or older students may have already mastered. In following the guidelines, the teacher or rehabilitation teacher needs to recognize that modifications should be made with adults to reflect their individual ability levels, needs, and wants. Indeed, to be successful, the approach must be individualized for every learner.

The first two steps in setting up a functional braille literacy program involve general assumptions or principles that are important considerations in this program as well as in any braille literacy program.

STEP 1

Determining the Primary Literacy Medium

LEARNING MEDIA ASSESSMENT

The first step in creating a functional braille literacy program for a learner is documenting that braille has actually been determined to be the learner's primary or secondary literacy medium by performing a learning media assessment. A learning media assessment involves using information from a functional vision evaluation, in addition to observing how the learner makes use of sensory information to determine whether braille will be recommended as a primary literacy medium either in place of or along with print. Although many factors are considered in a learning media assessment, primary factors include the amount of vision that a learner is able to use for reading and the stability of the eye condition. The most frequently used published learning media assessments available are those by Koenig and Holbrook (1995) and Sanford and Burnett (1997).

Learning media assessments also help determine how ready a learner is for a formal conventional (academic) or functional literacy program. Many of the at-risk learners described in the introduction, particularly those who have multiple disabilities, will not be considered candidates for a conventional literacy program. Indeed, based on the evaluation of literacy medium, these children will most likely be considered not ready, even for a functional literacy program. Despite their lack of readiness for a formal literacy program, however, it is still critical to know whether the learners are candidates for learning braille. These learners may remain in an emergent literacy stage for a much longer period of time than others who are learning to read more easily. Although print readers have ready access to print during emergent literacy stages, those for whom braille will be the medium do not have the same access to braille, since it is not generally available in the environment to the same degree. Without conscious efforts to expose these learners to braille, they may have only limited exposure to it or no knowledge that it exists at all. It is therefore critical to make the decision about the literacy medium early on, especially when the medium is to be braille, in order to be able to create the type of environment that will stimulate braille literacy, as described in Step 2.

UNCONTRACTED OR CONTRACTED BRAILLE?

Before moving to the next step in the program, however, the teacher also needs to determine whether the words will be introduced to the learner in uncontracted or contracted braille. Several factors make this decision a complicated one. (See the accompanying comparison of uncontracted and contracted braille.) Advantages to using contracted braille include the many short-form words and contractions that actually make it easier to read than reading letter by letter. For example, the alphabet letter words (*b* = *but; c* = *can; d* = *do,* etc.) can make reading faster and easier for students because they only have to read one letter that stands for an entire word. With the exception of *x* for *it* and *z* for *as,* these initial letter words can also help build phonics skills. Other contractions, such as *st, ch, ar, th,* and so on, also lend themselves nicely to learning phonics skills. Also, since braille signage in buildings and most published materials use contracted braille, learning contracted braille will give the individual access to environmental signs as well as to a wide body of literature.

The disadvantage to learning contracted braille is its complexity compared to uncontracted braille. Some contractions have multiple meanings in braille. A contraction can represent a whole word when the contraction is placed on the line with a space before and after it, or it can represent part of a word. For example, the contraction for *wh* stands for the word *which* and the contraction *en* stands for *enough* when these symbols have a space immediately before and after them. Put *wh* and *en* next to each other as part-word contractions, however, and they make the word

COMPARISON OF CONTRACTED AND UNCONTRACTED BRAILLE

As with any decision regarding a student's literacy program, the educational team needs to fully document and record the decision and the student's outcomes. A student can have success with either contracted or uncontracted braille—or a combination of both—if accurate records and assessments are kept and the student's progress is monitored. The following are key features that differentiate uncontracted and contracted braille:

Uncontracted Braille	Contracted Braille
With fewer rules for meaning of the same symbols in different contexts, uncontracted braille is less complex than contracted braille.	Many single symbols stand for whole words, so there are fewer characters to read.
A letter-for-letter translation of print words means fewer extra symbols to learn—just the alphabet and punctuation.	Contracted braille is the current standard for braille signage in the United States, so it is often found in the environment.
Learning uncontracted braille may help students in learning to spell, especially those who will learn keyboarding.	Some symbols can assist with the learning of phonics, especially symbols that stand for consonant digraphs (such as *st, th,* etc.).
Fewer symbols and rules to learn may increase the chances that family members and classroom teachers can learn braille and communicate with the student, and thus reinforce learning.	Currently, more reading material is available in contracted braille.
Current braille translation programs allow for production of materials in uncontracted braille.	Learning contractions from the beginning eliminates the need to relearn words and symbols later on.

when. Lower part- and whole-word symbols (those formed using only the lower four dots of the braille cell) can be confusing because they are similar in formation to upper symbols (those using only the upper four dots of the cell). For example, the dots 1-2-4-5 represent the letter *g* and the word *go*. The very same four-dot configuration using the lower dots 2-3-5-6 represents either the opening or closing parenthesis, depending on whether it is at the beginning or ending of a word; by itself, it represents the word *were.*

⠛ ⠶	go were
⠶⠓⠑ ⠗⠁⠝ ⠓⠕⠍⠑⠶	(he ran home)
⠶⠎⠕ ⠶ ⠽⠕⠥⠶	(so were you)

To those who learn to read braille as children and are introduced to these rules of usage through a variety of reading materials, braille does not seem any more difficult to learn than our antiquated spelling system for print seems to the ordinary print reader. But teachers often balk at introducing contracted braille to those for whom literacy is in question, especially for those learners who have mild to moderate cognitive impairments or learning impairments.

In actuality, learning contracted braille right from the beginning may be helpful to learners who have cognitive disabilities that make relearning material more difficult. Some educators feel that once a learner with cognitive disabilities recognizes a word in one form (such as the uncontracted form), it may be difficult for him or her to relearn it another way (as a contraction). In *Beginning with Braille,* Swenson (1999) provides a case study of a child named Eddie, a student with significant multiple disabilities, who was successful using simple contractions right from the beginning (e.g., *g = go, l = like*) because less tactile discrimination was required of him.

Today, braille translation software programs are capable of translating print into braille using only those contractions that have been introduced to the learner. Although this approach is generally not recommended by most educators for students following a traditional academic curriculum, a modified braille program for functional uses may be a good idea for those learners for whom some contractions are a good thing, but all the rules are too much. Teachers need to keep excellent records of which contractions the learner knows and which ones have yet to be learned. The learner may write using those contractions that have been learned and use uncontracted braille for those that have not yet been learned or are too confusing for the learner. Anna Swenson (personal communication, May 5, 2003) indicates that this approach is a viable option since many of the learners at this level are generally not reading vast quantities of braille, making it easy for a teacher to transcribe materials into braille using only the contractions the learner knows.

Adults or older learners who have already learned to read print can make the decision themselves about which form of braille to begin learning once they are informed of the various forms of the literary braille code. Some may prefer to use uncontracted braille so that they can learn to read and write familiar words again. Others may welcome the introduction of contracted braille, since it alleviates the need for having to read so many characters. Adults can make their own decision, as long as they are provided with the information about how the decision may limit their ability to read a wide variety of materials.

Although this brief discussion does not provide firm or fixed guidelines for determining whether to use contracted or uncontracted braille it should provide some basis for making the decision, other than just a "gut feeling." Whatever the decision, the teacher should be consistent in following through on it to give learners a chance to become accustomed to seeing words in that format.

STEP 2

Creating a Braille-Rich Environment

After determining that braille is to be the learner's literacy medium and determining whether contracted or uncontracted braille will be used, the second step is to examine the environment to see what access the learner has to braille reading and writing. The *Braille Literacy Curriculum* (Wormsley 2000) presents a framework for creating a braille-rich environment for school-aged learners that involves placing braille in the environment where a learner will be exposed to it, just as sighted learners are exposed to print. Sighted learners have constant exposure to their literacy medium—even though they may not yet be able to read it. Teachers expose sighted learners to print material even without having any expectations that they will be readers. When a sighted learner travels through a hallway, the teacher may point out the exit sign, the sign for the restrooms, or other print signs. The learner may not immediately recognize these words, but he or she is constantly being exposed to them. Without a conscious effort to put braille in the environment, that constant incidental exposure is not possible for a learner whose literacy medium will be braille.

The first step in creating a braille-rich environment is to examine the environment to decide where braille can be placed. Teachers can begin by looking to see where there is print in the rooms or hallways used by the learner. This can be done at home as well as in a school or rehabilitation setting.

It is important to recognize that many of the usual words taught to sighted learners may not be relevant for this process. For instance, for sighted learners with cognitive impairments, "exit" is a good word to learn to read. They learn where to look for it, how to recognize it, and that they can go to that exit in an emergency. However, the exit sign is most likely beyond the visual distance of a learner with a visual impairment, and if the individual is a braille reader, it is certainly beyond arm's reach. So, although the teacher can place signs such as the exit sign in braille in the environment, it is even more necessary to be creative and find other information that is in print and can be put in braille.

TEACHING ENVIRONMENTS

In a school or rehabilitation environment, the teacher can start by labeling the learner's immediate environment and possessions. For example, the learner's name can be written in braille on labels for his or her locker, desk, and other personal belongings. Other learners' names can also be in braille on their lockers, desks, and other possessions for the braille reader

A student's name in braille and print on a label for his desk.

to encounter. At home or in school, the words *on* and *off* on light switches can be labeled in braille as they are in print. *Hot* and *cold* can be labeled in braille on the water taps.

Some people advocate labeling furniture with braille labels. Although this doesn't really hurt anything, teachers want to be sure that children do not develop the idea that such objects have labels on them all the time. Sighted learners see labels around them at school but recognize that furniture is not labeled at home or in the community. Students with visual impairments do not have the wealth of visual experiences on which to base such judgments. Therefore, they often assume that the way they find things in one environment is the way they are everywhere. Telling them which kinds of objects generally are labeled and which are not is helpful.

A student's name on her locker in large print and in braille. The braille letter "k," representing her name, is also written with raised dots.

A light switch with "on" and "off" positions labeled in braille.

Organizational skills are extremely important for individuals with visual impairments to learn. Therefore, shelves should be organized so that students can get their own materials, with labels placed on the shelves in print and braille identifying what materials are there. Learners using a functional literacy approach are often in classes that focus on independent living skills. Labeling the equipment to be used, as well as where various utensils and supplies such as cutlery, dishes, and place mats are kept, will expose the learner to braille every time he or she sets the table for a meal or puts things away when cleaning up. Labeling materials in braille and keeping them in consistent places helps the learners to become more independent. Students who have never had sight learn that objects have a place in the environment—they don't just appear out of thin air.

The braille-rich environment should extend beyond the learner's classroom into the entire school or rehabilitation setting. Wherever the learner goes, he or she should be exposed to braille. The teacher might want to start by providing braille labels in the learner's classroom, and then gradually expand farther and farther away from it. In this way, the teacher can

Braille signage on a restroom.

provide braille in the environment without being overwhelmed by trying to perform the task all at once. For instance, after all the appropriate items in the classroom have been labeled in braille, the teacher can work on the corridor outside the classroom. Where there is print, there can be braille. Teachers' names are often on their rooms, as are their room numbers. Restrooms usually have braille signage already on them. There are usually signs that point visitors to various places when they enter the building. Braille the sign for the main office, administrators' offices, nurse's office, cafeteria, library, and any other rooms or locations with signs that can be transcribed into braille and placed alongside the print and where they are reachable. Teachers can expose learners to these signs when traveling from class to class or on mobility lessons.

Learners who are visually impaired are often included in music class, since they can participate in singing by memorizing the words. They may have no idea that reading is involved, however, both in the sense of reading the words and reading the music. Providing the braille reader with the materials that sighted students have in print is important, even if the learner is not yet able to read them. If the learner is participating in music class, he or she should know that reading is part of that experience.

HOME ENVIRONMENT

The home environment is not intrinsically a "teaching environment," as is a school, although it is certainly a "learning environment." However, teachers can work with parents to help provide a braille-rich environment at home as well as in school. If parents do not know braille, teachers may create the labels for the parents for their home environments and add print to them so the parents will know to which items or locations the labels belong. Teachers can discuss with the parents how to provide models of reading and writing for their child. (See Role Models, below). Creating a braille-rich environment in the home of an adult client requires a little more sensitivity. To adults, their home is their dominion. In creating a braille-rich environment for adults, rehabilitation teachers must first establish rapport with their clients and make sure that they are motivated to have braille in their environment. Adult learners can then choose to be involved in creating braille labels for their home. At the same time that the rehabilitation teacher may be teaching adults to use a labeling system with raised markings for items on which labels are essential (such as medications or stove markings), the learner who has decided that he or she wants to learn to read braille may be deciding what items are familiar enough to be recognized by touch or smell. These items can then be labeled in braille. Touching the braille labels on items that are used constantly familiarizes the adult learner with the feel of the braille, and since the label is on something familiar, he or she will know what the braille says and get used to the shape of the specific word. Spices in the spice cabinet that can be identified by smell, or familiar sayings on plaques on the walls (I have one in my house that says "Come in, sit down, relax, converse. My house doesn't always look like this. Sometimes it's even worse!") are good candidates for braille labels to expose the learner to braille. This step of creating a braille-rich environment may have to be delayed for a while if the adult learner is resistant to learning braille. If that is the case, the rehabilitation teacher may wish to skip and go directly to Step 3 with this learner, in which the learner chooses the words he or she might have the necessity or desire to read in braille. Sometimes, having success with one or two words in braille is what motivates the older learner to want to learn more. A rehabilitation teacher will be sensitive to this and not insist on brailling objects in the adult learner's environment until the learner is ready and motivated to do more with braille.

WORK ENVIRONMENT

For learners who have jobs or work-experience opportunities outside of their main classroom, the work tasks may provide opportunities for exposure to braille. Students may deliver the local newspaper. The rooms to which the newspaper will be delivered can be identified with braille as well as print. A task such as packaging plastic cutlery may involve retrieving the cutlery from several bins. The bins in which the various items are contained can be labeled in braille to identify the items being retrieved. "Spoon," "fork," and "knife" are meaningful items that should have braille symbols paired with them. The purpose of providing the braille is not for the learner to immediately learn to read the words, but for the learner to realize that spoken words have written counterparts. Since these

The word "newspaper" in braille and large-print letters, paired with a miniature rolled-up newspaper, signifies where a newspaper should be delivered.

words have meaning to the learner, they could at some point become part of his or her personal reading and writing vocabulary. These words are now functional for the learner at work.

Other job tasks may associate a name with a number—for instance, the task of packaging plumbing parts. The part name *bolt* can be paired with a number indicating how many bolts must be retrieved from the bolt box. This pairing may help the learner to realize that words can be more than just the names of objects—they can also relate, in this example, to numbers.

Putting braille in the environment is only the first step. Since it is harder for a person who is visually impaired to find braille on an object than it is for a sighted person to find print, teachers, parents, and other caregivers need to show the learner where the braille is located and explain what it means. For example, putting a student's name on his or her locker is a good way to start, but the learner must be informed that it is there and be reminded to check for the name label when the locker is used. The learner needs to be informed of the location of the braille word and to encounter it repeatedly in different contexts. This applies to all the places where braille is placed in the environment. Thus, positioning of the braille material to be read is extremely important. A learner must have physical access to the braille, and the braille needs to be placed where the learner can reach it and where he or she can read it by touch. Eye level is not necessarily touch level.

ROLE MODELS

In addition to not having as much exposure to braille as a reading medium as their sighted counterparts do to print, potential braille readers also do not have as much exposure to role models of people reading and writing braille. Sighted people can look around them to see role models of people using print to read and write. Therefore, the braille-rich environment also needs to contain examples of people using braille for a wide range of tasks and purposes. For example, teachers can create notes for others using a Perkins brailler or a slate and stylus, and ask the braille reader to deliver them (this is also a good purpose for a mobility lesson on independent travel). Print-braille books are a necessity and are becoming more widely available (see the Resources Section). Print-braille books have both print and the corresponding braille on their pages. This permits print readers to read the books while braille readers follow along, or braille readers can read the books and show the pictures and print to print readers. These books allow parents to help their braille-reading children with difficult words, something that isn't possible when the book contains just braille. For learners who are not yet reading and yet are older than typical beginning readers, finding print-braille books that are age-appropriate may be a problem. Setting a goal for these older students to read simple stories from print-braille books to younger children may provide motivation for them to practice reading something that is obviously designed for young children. Using a language experience approach, as suggested later, to create books in both print and braille may be another solution.

To summarize, it is extremely important that the learner's environment be modified to include the medium in which he or she will read and write. The purpose of the braille-rich environment is to develop the concept of what reading consists of and where it occurs. Learners who are going to be braille readers need more exposure to where reading occurs, and more exposure to braille, not less. The typical environment simply does not support the learning of braille in the way that it supports the learning of print. As Kliewer and Landis (1999) state, "As educators, we must surround all children with a symbolic and literate milieu, and facilitate their participation therein with thoughtful resources, activities and expectations" (p. 99).

The ideas mentioned in Steps 1 and 2 apply to all learners for whom braille is to be the primary literacy medium, whether they will be in a conventional or a functional literacy program. The remaining steps are highly individualized in the functional literacy program.

STEP 3

Selecting the Individualized Reading and Writing Vocabulary

The next step—and truly the heart of the functional approach to braille literacy—is to select the words that will be used in initial instruction with individual learners. The more meaningful these words are to the learners, the more motivated they will be to learn to read. As described in the Introduction, when Warner (1963) asked her Maori children to pick the words they wanted to learn to read, she discovered that the first words they wanted to learn to read were the words that were the most emotionally laden for them. These words were the ones they learned most quickly and remembered most easily.

Creating a braille-rich environment will help the learner develop the concept of what reading and writing braille is all about if they do not already have this concept. But learners may not see reading and writing braille as relevant or motivating if the initial symbols they learn to read are meaningless or of no interest to them. It is critical to discover what is important to learners and especially the specific words used to refer to these important things when selecting this initial vocabulary. For example, if the learner has a dog that is a favorite pet, it is important to find out what word is used when referring to dogs in general. Is it *puppy? Mutt? Doggin?* What is the dog's name? Is it *Zeke? Nicky? Spot?* The word *dog* may not elicit any degree of interest, whereas *puppy* and *Nicky* may elicit happy emotions if these are the words the learner associates with this favorite pet.

First the teacher collects the vocabulary words. If learners are verbal, like Warner's Maori children, they can tell the teacher the words they want to learn. However, when trying to create stories (see Step 10), teachers may need more than the words the learners provide. Therefore, while it is initially sufficient to use a few words suggested by the learner, it is important to collect a lot of words that are relevant and meaningful.

Older learners are usually very motivated to list the words they want to read. A high school student may want to read friends' telephone numbers or CD titles or the color labels on makeup. Adult homemakers may want to read labels on spices or the names of grandchildren. The key is to ask the learner to provide you, the teacher, with the words that are the most important to him or her.

Some learners may be less verbal than others, but may still be able to hear words used in the environment and understand these words, even if they are not able to tell the teacher what words they want to learn. With this type of learner, it is essential that the teacher find out what words are used frequently with the learner. The chart in Figure 1 provides a vehicle for collecting vocabulary words from the home, school or rehabilitation setting, and community environments for those children who are not able to express themselves verbally.

When using this tool, it is important to understand that *words* are being collected, not just information, although teachers may also discover a wealth of useful information they did not know about learners as they begin to collect these words. Rehabilitation teachers can also use this form for their adult learners. If the learners are verbal, rehabilitation teachers may be able to elicit vocabulary words from all areas of the environment during a single question and answer session.

Collecting vocabulary words with learners, especially if they are non-verbal, is time-consuming. Teachers may want to start examining the

FIGURE 1: Sample Form for Collecting Initial Vocabulary Words

WORDS IN LEARNER'S ENVIRONMENT

Questions for Gathering Vocabulary	Rehabilitation/ or School Setting	Home Setting	Community
What are the names of significant people with whom the learner interacts?			
What are the words used to describe the learner's daily routine?			
What are the names of the learner's hobbies, favorite things, and favorite activities?			
What are the words used to describe the learner's work activities or chores?			

Source: Adapted with permission of the publisher from D. P. Wormsley, *Braille Literacy Curriculum,* coypright © 2000, Towers Press, Overbrook School for the Blind, Philadelphia, PA.

school or rehabilitation environment, where the most information will be available, and then solicit the help of family members for the home and community portions of the chart. The following is a description of how to use the chart with children; the process can be readily adapted into an interview format for use with adults.

The first question on the chart deals with people with whom the learner interacts. A child will most likely interact with the teacher, classroom aide, other students, people in the cafeteria, therapists, and so on. The task is to write down the *names* that the child uses to refer to these people. For instance, the mobility instructor may be Mr. Conchetta, but the student may call him "Mr. C." *Mr. C.* would then become the vocabulary word to use in reading and writing, rather than *Mr. Conchetta.*

The second question refers to the learner's daily routine. Examples of vocabulary words to include would be the names of places where he or she goes during the day (*cafeteria, bus, gymnasium*), as well as scheduled activities (*music, cooking, physical education* or *gym, library, lunch*). There will be favorite foods on the menu at the cafeteria (*macaroni and cheese, tomato soup, lasagna, coke, chocolate milk*). There will be the names of items in the classroom used for reading and writing or for other activities (*brailler, slate and stylus, tape recorder, paper, locker, desk, chair*). All these become meaningful vocabulary words to be used in a functional approach to teaching braille literacy.

The third area where vocabulary words can be found is in the area of hobbies, favorite things, or favorite activities. The teacher can list vocabulary words for what the student especially enjoys doing in school. Some words selected for a student with whom this approach was used include *radio,* for listening to the radio; *Pepsi,* for walking to the soda machine to buy a soft drink; and *tapes,* for listening to music on the tape recorder.

The final area of the chart, refers to classroom chores or work activities that a student does during the school day as well as chores at home or actual employment for an adult. A student may help deliver the school newspaper or have a prevocational job that has additional vocabulary words associated with it. Again, the words selected should be the actual terms used when making reference to these jobs. The phrase *deliver the newspaper* will have meaning to the child who does that job. *Pre-voc* is the term used in his school for work experiences or activities during the school day. The words that are used when on the job may also be part of the vocabulary; for example, *Pizza Hut, pizza, boxes,* and *fold,* might be vocabulary words selected for a student who works off campus to fold boxes at the local pizzeria.

To collect words from the home and community environments, the teacher should interview the family members and other caretakers who know the child well. A caretaker can often add to the vocabulary words. The words selected should be the names the child uses to refer to the most important people in his or her home and community environment. The child may interact with parents, grandparents, and siblings in the home environment. However, just as in the classroom, the words selected should be what the child *calls* these people (*Mom, Daddy, Nanna, Poppa, Jen,* and *Bo,* for instance). Teachers can identify the relationships to the child in parentheses on the chart if the relationships are not obvious. (For example, *Nanna* may be the mother's mother, whereas *Grandma* may be the father's mother.) These names can be some of the child's first reading words, along with his or her own name.

Interviewing the family about the daily routine may provide a host of words or phrases to use, such as *Hurry up! Eat your breakfast,* or *Eat your eggs.* Phrases that the family uses frequently with the child at home are what the teacher needs to capture, even if the student does not say them. Talking with the family about the daily routine may also provide names of others who are important to the child to add under the first part of the chart— people with whom the child interacts. Perhaps asking the family about the daily routine will remind them of the bus driver, Mr. Ned, or another child who rides the bus. The interview will provide insight into what the child likes and dislikes about the daily routine, which will help the teacher make choices of when to use which words. Sometimes children will tell everyone what they like. Less expressive children may have difficulty supplying these words. This is why the family interview is so important.

Along with the daily routine, teachers can ask about things the family does on the weekend. Do they go to Nanna's house regularly for dinner? Do they go to church or temple? Do they take walks? Do they go shopping? Do they do chores around the house? The child may enjoy accompanying the family on outdoor activities, or to a fast food restaurant on a weekly basis. When talking to families about their normal routines, avoid making value judgements about the activities they choose. What is in the family's experience will be meaningful to the child—whether it is interesting to someone else is not important in the context of selecting these vocabulary words.

If the child is unable to supply the words for favorite hobbies, items, or activities, family members can be asked to provide the name of the child's favorite song, musician, television show, game, food, toy, or activity. For example, one child has a favorite blanket called "Binky," another has a favorite doll named "Sue," and another has a favorite pet rabbit named "Ears." The names are the important thing to collect, but the teacher should also put a description of the item or object to which the name refers in parentheses to help the teacher remember that "Ears" is the rabbit and "Sue" is the doll.

The final area to ask about is work activities or chores. Some students may not have chores at home. Others may be expected to participate in some activity and teachers should know what that activity is. Does the family refer to *chores* or *duties* or *jobs?* The specific names of the chores should also be captured: *taking out the garbage, emptying wastebaskets,* and so on. The more specific the information collected, the more individualized the reading vocabulary becomes.

After the teacher has collected the vocabulary words in each of the environments, favorite expressions that the child uses may be recorded. The student is familiar with them and understands what they mean when they are used. Sometimes a greeting used by a favorite teacher brings a smile to a child's face every time he or she hears it. As an example, when Mr. C. comes into the classroom and says, "Yo, buddy!" Jimmy's face lights up, and he knows that it is time for his mobility lesson. This expression will be fun for the student to learn to read.

Using the chart helps create a set of words or phrases for beginning reading. The words collected through this process represent the most important words for the learner at this point in time. They are his or her functional vocabulary to use as the basis for many entertaining stories, games, and activities, which the teacher and child can develop together as the child is beginning to learn to read and write braille.

In using the chart with verbal adults, the rehabilitation teacher may wish to do this in a manner similar to the way the interview is conducted with the parents of a child, but instead to do the interview with the adult client. In addition, the adult may have some specific goals for literacy that he or she wishes to attain which can also be the basis for some of the initial words and lessons. The words may derive from those goals.

For example, if an adult homemaker wants to be able to create a grocery shopping list with the staples that she normally purchases that she can read herself, the names of those staples could become the words to write down on the chart under daily routines for the home. Numbers may even be chosen, if the learner wishes to be able to read telephone numbers. The rehabilitation teacher can extend the interview to include names of family members and friends which the learner would want to read.

With adults who are not native English speakers, it might be necessary to have a translator on hand for the interview, and to translate the key words into English. The subsequent lessons will most likely serve the dual purpose of teaching braille and English at the same time. At the beginning of working with a learner, student or adult, 20 to 30 words will be sufficient. The teacher or rehabilitation teacher can collect more and these initial vocabulary words can be added to as the learner becomes successful in recognizing them.

STEP 4

Creating Word Boxes and Flash Cards and Teaching the First Key Words

Once the learner's reading and writing vocabulary has been listed, the teacher and learner, whether child or adult, can decide together the first words to use in the functional literacy program. These will become the learner's key words and each will be brailled on an individual flash card to use in teaching the learner to read his or her own functional vocabulary. The flash cards are stored in the learner's word box.

MAKING THE WORD BOX AND FLASH CARDS

The word box contains flash cards that have the words chosen by a particular learner brailled on them. The word box can be identified with the learner's name brailled on it and can be decorated to make it tactilely distinct with such things as Wikki Stiks (waxy, bendable pipe cleaners) or raised stickers. The mode for decorating should be the learner's choice. Teachers might use the creation of the word box as an enjoyable art project that will also help the learner develop his or her fine motor skills. Adults may choose a simple container such as a plastic storage box.

The words should be brailled on card stock of a consistent size, such as index cards. Generally, braille flash cards have the top right-hand corner cut off on an angle, which allows a braille reader to know how to position the card for reading. Instead of having just one word in the center of a card, it is preferable to have a lead-in line of dots 2-5 with a space before the word and a space after, followed by a line of dots 2-5 leading away from the word. Using lead-in lines allows the reader to locate the word on the flash card while keeping the fingers moving from left to right, so as to discourage scrubbing, (moving the finger up and down over the

The word box used to hold the learner's word cards can be a simple plastic container or it can be decorated, as the learner chooses.

braille dots) which slows down the reader. Using the middle dots 2-5 for lead-in lines also centers the fingertips and provides a frame of reference for the position of the dots in what follows it. Learners can eventually be weaned from using these lines, but initially the longer the lead-in lines the better, as it encourages smooth left to right tracking over the word. (Cards should be as large as possible to encourage the proper tracking of the word—smaller than 3" × 5" will not encourage proper tracking.)

Several types of cards can be used for making flash cards.

- 3" × 5" index cards or 4" × 6" index cards

- Blank flash cards available for purchase from the American Printing House for the Blind, which come with a corner already cut off.

- Cards that have magnetic strips attached such as those used with talking card readers.

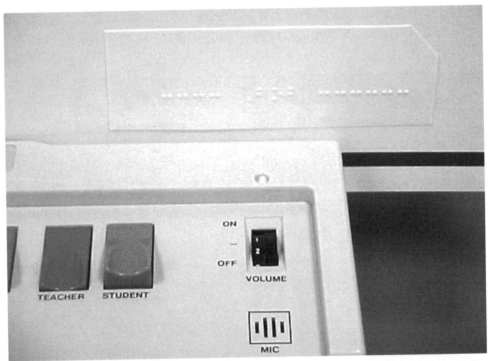

A flash card with lead-in and lead-out lines incorporated onto a card with a magnetic strip for use with a talking card reader.

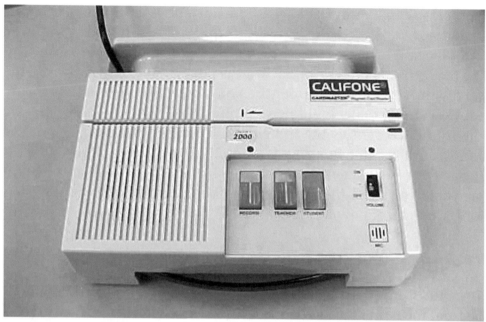

A talking card reader.

Talking card readers, such as the Cardmaster, VoxCom, and Language Master use cards with magnetic strips attached. The teacher can record a brief message on the card's magnetic tape strip to match the word or phrase that is in braille on the card. Once learners have been taught how to use the cards and the machine to play back the messages, they can check their accuracy in reading by first reading the braille on the card, and then playing the card in the machine to see whether they read it correctly.

Teachers should make one flash card for the box for each word in the learner's functional vocabulary and then make many extras of each word so that the learner can see the word more than once. Remember that when sighted learners read flash cards, they get to see the cards for an extended period of time. Braille readers should be able to read a flash card over and over until they can decide what the word is, and they should have multiple opportunities for determining what the word is.

The word box will become the storage container for all the words a learner identifies, and the word cards will be placed in the box as the learner is able to recognize them. Care must be taken when placing the word cards in the word box to allow learners to read the words while the cards are still in the box. By placing the word cards upside down with the braille facing toward the back of the box, a reader can easily read the card without removing it from the box. Some may wonder how many words you eventually build up to. This will depend upon how quickly the learner recognizes the individual words, and whether or not the words become automatic and used in more extensive reading and writing activities. As students begin to use phonics skills to decode unfamiliar words, the use of the word box may be gradually decreased if it is no longer needed or desired.

TEACHING AND LEARNING THE FIRST KEY WORDS

Once the word box is prepared, and the first key word has been identified and the flash cards made, the learner needs to be taught how to position the card for reading in order to become independent in the use of the word box. Using a nonslip material under the card (a material called Dycem or a mat made of rubberized shelf liner work well) allows the learner to read the card with both hands and helps keep the card in place. As noted, the flash card will have a slice off the top right-hand corner that will help the learner place it right side up. Once the learner has the card positioned correctly on the mat, the teacher should show the learner how to track along the lead-in lines to find the word and then how to keep the fingers moving over the word to find the lead-out lines. The learner should be encouraged to keep the pads of all four fingers of both hands on the line of braille with the index fingers positioned next to each other. That gives the reader a span of eight fingers. The more fingers that are in contact with the braille line, the more information the reader receives, although only one or two, generally the index fingers will actually identify characters. The other fingers may act as "scouts" to determine how long a word or line is, or to maintain contact with the line so the fingers don't slip off that line and onto another by mistake. It is important to talk to the learner about finger placement on the line and to observe to see whether the learner has any difficulty with hand and finger position.

Next the teacher helps the learner to tactilely identify the word. Knowing what the word is before it is encountered will help the learner keep fingers moving across it while telling the teacher what the word is. Since the student has chosen or is familiar with the word, he or she will be more likely to be able to tell the teacher what the word is. If not, the teacher should identify it for the student. Once the learner feels the word several times, the teacher should talk to the learner about how the word feels and point out its unique features. For example, if the word is long, the teacher can discuss this with the learner. With some learners, the teacher can point out whether the dots at the beginning of the word are at the top, middle, or bottom so that learners can become accustomed to thinking in this fashion. For example, in the word *cat,* the word starts out with dots all at the top, above the lead-in line, and then ends with dots in the top, middle, and bottom positions. This analysis of word features may be how the learner identifies words initially, but the teacher will gradually begin

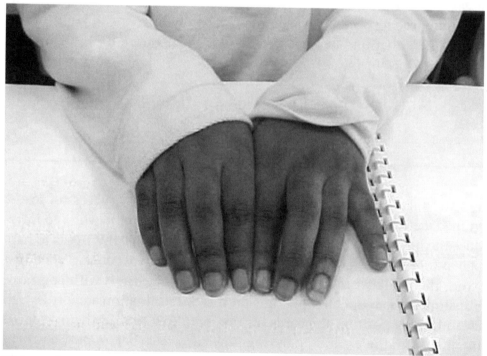

This student is practicing keeping her fingers in a line when reading braille.

to introduce the individual letters at the beginning of these words to use in word recognition as well. Some learners may already be able to identify a letter at the beginning of the word during this activity if they have had some braille instruction previously.

Some learners may need an additional activity to help them focus on the word as being different from the lead-in lines. To do this, the teacher can create a blank word card with lines of dots 2-5 at the beginning and end of the line and a blank space where the word would go. Using this card along with the key word card, the teacher can help the student understand whether there is a word on the card or just a blank space. This can help the learner understand which part of the flash card to focus on.

It is important that words become overlearned before starting to learn another word. Discussions related to how the word looks or feels are important in this overlearning. Swenson (1999) suggests introducing the learner's name first and then a group of five unspaced full cells as their second "word," which is called "Mr. Nobody." The learner can then play a game to differentiate his or her own name from "Mr. Nobody." This gives the teacher an idea of whether or not the learner can perform this gross differentiation task, and the kids get a kick out of it!

John   "Mr. Nobody"

Introducing only one word will make the learner a successful reader immediately. Therefore, the next decision is to determine when to introduce the next word. For some older students and adults, this needs to happen as soon as they are able to recognize the difference between their first word, the blank word card, and "Mr. Nobody." Learners with cognitive impairments may spend more time on this discrimination activity as well as on how to position the cards on the mat, how to read them, reading them over and over, and analyzing how each feels before putting them away in the word box.

When introducing the second word, the teacher can follow the same procedure as with the first word. The teacher should tell the learner what the word is and then have the learner track across the lead-in line, locate the word, and read it. The teacher and student can discuss how the word feels and compare it to the first word learned and to "Mr. Nobody." It helps if the second word is tactilely distinct from the first word, that is, the word is noticeably different in length or letter configuration. The teacher can ask questions such as, "Is this word longer than your other word?" "Shorter?" "Where are the dots at the beginning of the word?" "At the end?" "Is there anything you feel that stands out to you?" How the learner responds can help the teacher understand what he or she needs to point out about the word. If the learner is not able to answer the questions, the teacher should model the process providing the answers.

The teacher can then introduce a simple discrimination game to determine how well the learner can tactilely discriminate between both word cards. Mr. Nobody and the blank word card can also be included. The teacher will already have multiple cards brailled for each word, so that the learner doesn't use irrelevant features of the card (such as a rough spot on the right side of the card, for example) to discriminate one word from another.

Learners can also learn to separate flash cards into two piles: those that were read correctly in one pile, and those that were read incorrectly in another. Learners can be taught to use a magnetic card reader to check their own reading and to separate the correctly read words from the others. Having containers available for the two sets of cards is helpful. After a learner demonstrates that he or she can independently separate the cards that were read correctly and incorrectly, this can become a daily activity, and the teacher can examine the piles the learner creates for a record of success and as a potential for diagnostic teaching (discussed in Step 11). Practicing each word until it is recognized automatically is an important sign of mastery. The greater variety of games that a teacher can create to allow word reading and recognition, the better. Swenson (personal communication, May 5, 2003) suggests some additional types of matching games:

- Sorting flash cards into two or more groups (for example, using a set of 10 cards, 5 with one word and 5 with another)

- Matching flash cards (e.g., on a teacher-made board with library card pockets or Velcro)

- Keeping track of how many flash cards a student can recognize accurately in one minute

For a rehabilitation teacher who is using the functional literacy approach with adults, the magnetic card reader can be extremely useful. The rehabilitation teacher may meet with an adult client only once or twice a week. If clients are capable and motivated, the rehabilitation teacher may be able to teach the adult how to use the magnetic card reader to check reader accuracy and leave the machine and a set of word cards brailled on the magnetic strip cards with the learner. Adults who are also learning to write braille (and may have more capability in that arena than in reading) may create key word cards for themselves and use the recording feature of the magnetic card reader to record the word immediately after they have brailled it. This will also permit them to expand the number of words that they can recognize independently.

The pace for introducing new words has to be set by the learner's abilities with the words previously introduced. Routman (2003) writes that we must "teach with a sense of urgency, . . . making every moment in the classroom count, . . . ensuring that our instruction engages students and moves them ahead, . . . using daily evaluation and reflection to make wise teaching decisions" (p. 41). So, it is important to introduce new words as soon as possible. The teacher can start by attempting to introduce a new word on a daily basis and assess how well the learner is discriminating this word from the others learned. Each day the word recognition is accurate for all the words, the teacher can introduce a new word. If this pace is too fast for the learner and he or she cannot recognize new words easily, the teacher can decrease the rate at which the words are introduced. The teacher should keep a record of the words introduced and the words recognized. The true test of whether a learner has mastered a word is independence. The learner should be able to do the sorting task accurately, without the teacher close by, and without prompts (A. Swenson, personal communication, May 5, 2003).

Warner (1963) felt that if her Maori students didn't learn the words almost immediately, then the words were not motivating enough for the students. At that point, she would remove them from their word boxes. In any event, the teacher needs to continue to have learners select new words for reading and to introduce them in the same way as the previous words were introduced—by using flash cards discussing how the words feel, and comparing them to the words learned previously. At the same time, the teacher will begin to introduce the next step of the functional approach to braille literacy: that of teaching tactile perception skills.

STEP 5

Teaching Tactile Perception and Letter-Recognition Skills through Tracking Activities

When the learner has at least two words in his or her Word Box that have been successfully discriminated with at least 90 percent accuracy, it is time to introduce tracking exercises that make use of the words and to begin selecting individual letters from those words to use in teaching accurate letter identification.

TRACKING ACTIVITIES

Tracking skills (maintaining contact with the braille line while reading braille) should not be separated from perception and letter-recognition skills in teaching braille reading. Learners can easily be taught smooth tracking skills on braille lines without being asked to recognize any of the characters. Their smooth tracking, however, deteriorates when character recognition is introduced into the task (Wormsley, 1979). To be able to read while keeping the fingers moving from left to right across the characters demands that the characters be automatically recognized by the fingertips. Beginning readers must consciously keep their fingers moving from left to right over the characters and may struggle to identify the letters. They may have to go back to the beginning of the line and start again. As braille character recognition develops, however, it is the recognition of the individual letters or words that actually drives the fingers onward. Movement is necessary for tactile recognition to occur (Kusajima, 1974; Millar, 1997). Learners who are not taught to identify characters while moving their fingers smoothly over them from left to right will develop the habit of moving the fingertip up and down on characters to assist in recognition. This behavior, termed *scrubbing,* detracts from speed in reading and must be addressed at the beginning of reading instruction. Almost all braille readers will attempt to scrub at one point or another. They are telling the teacher that they are unable to recognize the letters underneath their fingers and that they know that they need to identify the character before moving on.

Teachers will need to develop materials for tracking and accurate character recognition. A program that is designed for just this purpose is *The Mangold Developmental Program of Tactile Perception and Braille Letter Recognition* (Mangold, 1989). This program is designed to develop good tracking and hand movement skills while also teaching learners to identify all the letters of the alphabet. Because the functional approach uses an individual vocabulary and draws the letters to be identified from key words that the student already knows, it may not be possible to follow the Mangold program exactly as it is designed, but the program can give a teacher suggestions for useful activities to incorporate into the functional approach.

A useful beginning activity involves a full sheet of lines composed of dots 2-5 that are double- or triple-spaced. This serves as the baseline against which to measure the other characters a learner will encounter, since some braille letters contain dots 1-4, which would be above this line, and some have dots 3-6, which would be below it. Some educators advocate using lines of full cells instead of dots 2-5. One reason for using dots 2-5 instead of full cells is that the student's fingers will not "numb out" (that is, become desensitized), as quickly with just dots 2-5. Once students are more sensitized to braille, using lines of full cells in future lessons will not be a problem. Beginner's fingers do become desensitized rather quickly so be sure to take finger breaks every five minutes or so initially and gradually increase the time span for tracking.

The learner begins by tracking the lines with both hands together and the index fingers touching on the sides. Both hands should stay close together with all four of the fingers of each hand in contact with the line. This means that the student may have to curve his or her fingers in order to maintain contact with the braille line. The teacher will need to closely observe the learner in this initial phase of tracking to monitor the hands and fingers. Learners may decide that this is difficult for them. They need to be encouraged to keep trying to use all four fingers of each hand and to keep both hands close together. The teacher may want to use a pencil or other straight edge to demonstrate to the learner whether the fingers are lined up or not. Teachers can also use a guided reading technique where the teacher's left thumb and fingers create a "frame" that rests above and to the left of the learner's fingers as he or she reads. The teacher's thumb can gently push the learner fingers along as they track the line of braille together.

Adults and older students will need less assistance, but students who are cognitively impaired may need a systematic way of helping them find the first line of braille to track. Pages should have the top right-hand corner cut off, similar to the way corners are cut off on the flash cards, so that the learner may independently position the paper on the nonslip surface. The learner should be taught to move his or her hands to the top left-hand side of the page, and then to move down until the braille is reached. At this point, the learner may begin tracking the first line of dots 2-5 from the beginning of the line and continue until the end is reached.

Having the learner use both hands initially allows the learner to feel the braille moving under both hands. This is preferable to beginning with a method that would encourage reading with only the right hand, such as the method in which the left hand is used as a marker and the right hand does all the reading. Using both hands allows for the fingers of both hands to become sensitized and to have equal exposure to the braille. That way, if one hand is more dominant it will possibly take the lead. Students for whom the left index finger is more sensitive to reading braille will be able to benefit from the use of the left hand in reading. It is also a good idea to have each hand read separately from time to time, to be sure that both hands are learning to discriminate braille words and letters. If one hand is less sensitive, extra practice with that hand alone may be helpful.

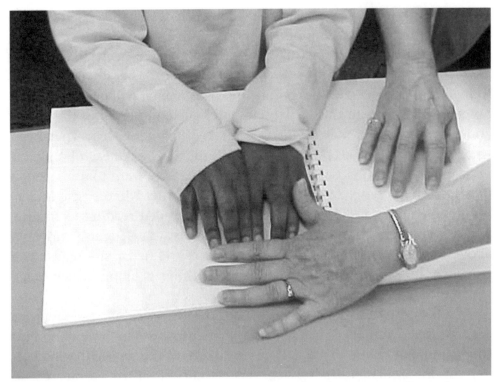

A teacher assisting a student to properly position fingers on a line of braille by creating a "frame" with her left hand.

The teacher may even want to create games in which the hands "compete" against each other! (A. Swenson, May 5, 2003).

Once the learner is able to stay on a line of braille from beginning to end without "falling off," it is time to teach him or her how to move down to the next line. There are two different ways to teach a learner how to do this. The first method involves having the learner move both hands together down to the next line. The learner moves both hands together back across the line just tracked and then moves the hands together down to locate the next line and tracks across it. This method is generally easier for beginners. The second method is to have the learner leave the right hand at the end of the line just tracked, move the left hand back across that line to the beginning and then down to locate the next line. Once that next line is found, the learner can move the right hand to join the left before they take off again to track the line together. Teachers may want to start with both hands together and then evaluate the capabilities of the learner to separate the hands at the end of the line before attempting to introduce the latter method. Separating the hands allows for more efficient braille reading.

When the learner can track several triple-spaced braille lines composed of dots 2-5, the teacher can begin to introduce some simple recognition skills into the tracking. Lamb (1996) and Swenson (1999) have some good suggestions on how to design tracking activities that are meaningful for students. An easy way to do this involves placing the first key word that the learner knows somewhere in each line of dots 2-5, but in a different location on each line. The teacher can then set up some meaningful scenarios around the use of this word. Set the scenario for the tracking activities based on activities that the learner enjoys. This is where the interviews and information about hobbies and favorite activities will come in handy.

For example, if Bob's first word was his name, and Bob likes swimming, the scenario might be that the lines of dots 2-5 represent the water in the pool and his name represents where he is in the swimming pool (see Figure 2). Bob is asked to track across the lines to see how far out in the water he is. When he reaches his name (separated from the lines of 2-5 by a space on either side), he is to say his name aloud and continue tracking to the end of the line. The placement of Bob's name on the lines should be staggered from one line to the next so the teacher can see whether he is able to find his name on each line.

Initially, it is important to remind the learner to keep his or her fingers moving when the learner reaches his or her name. Using a word that is already familiar to the learner, and letting him or her know what that word is will be helpful in this activity.

In the initial stages of learning, teachers must monitor learners closely during extensive tracking practice, since learners' fingers may become numb without their recognizing the sensation. What learners will feel will be a general lessening of sensitivity to the braille characters, and they will begin making errors or say they can't recognize characters when they have previously done well. Learners need to recognize that numbness may occur unless they take short "finger breaks." Let the learner massage fin-

FIGURE 2: **Bob Swimming in the Pool**

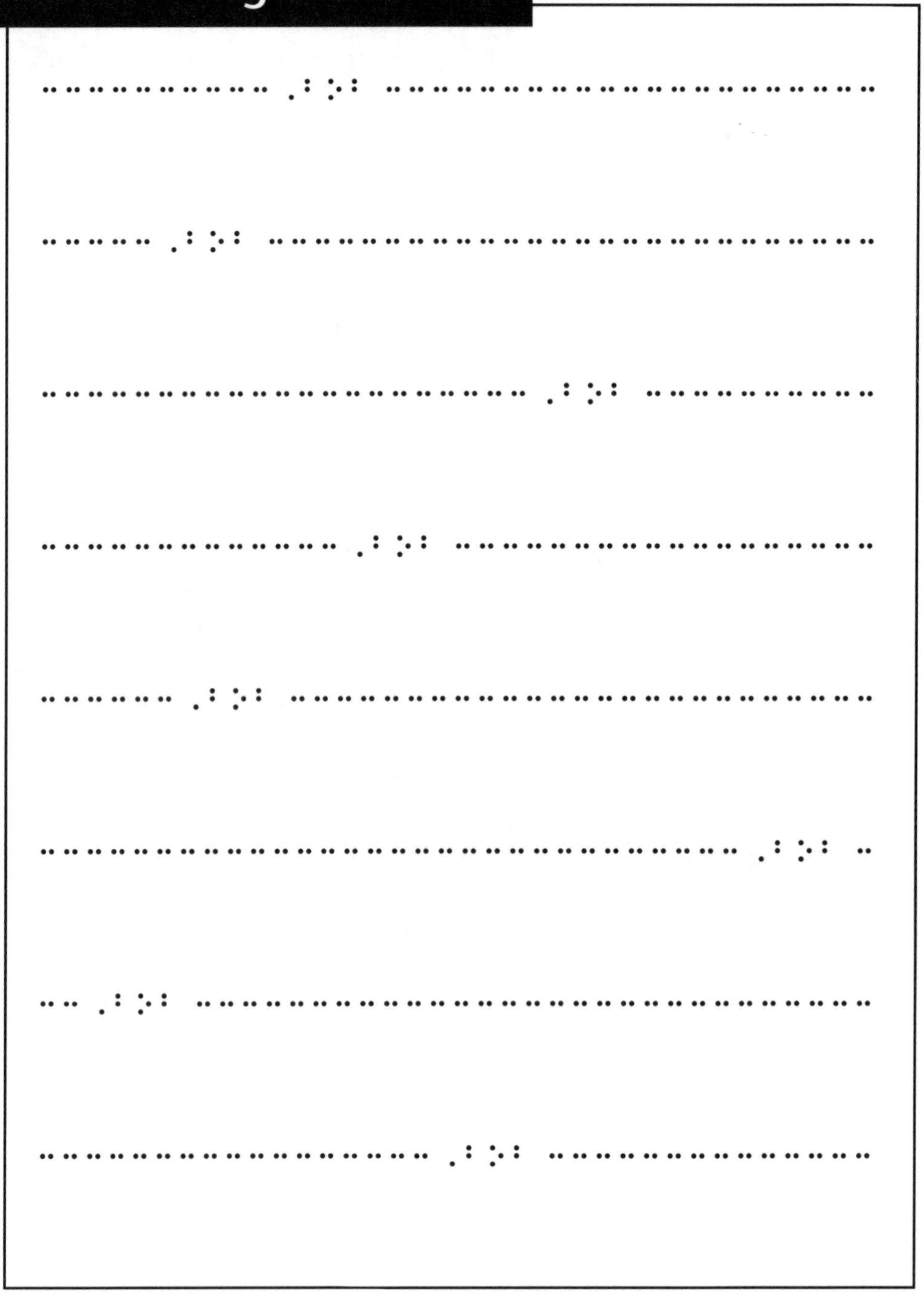

gers and hands with hand cream, or perhaps switch to another activity for a few minutes.

Once the learner has been able to track successfully, and can accurately identify the first key word when it occurs in braille, it is time to use the second key word in the tracking exercises. Again, depending on what this word is, the teacher may be able to set up a scenario around both words. For example, if Jean's two key words are her name and *Spot,* her dog's name, and she likes to go walking with Spot, the first scenario might be that she is walking to Spot's kennel in the backyard so they can take a walk together (a page of lines of dots 2-5 with the word *Jean* in various places). The second scenario might be that Spot has gotten away, and she must find him on the sidewalk (a page of lines of dots 2-5 with the word *Spot* in various places). Once Jean can track and identify the two names individually, it is time to have both names on the line. The scenario could be that Jean is trying to find Spot. Jean must track the lines and find *Jean* and *Spot* on each line. This page could consist of lines of dots 2-5 with the words *Jean* and *Spot* on the lines in various places, sometimes with *Jean* on the left side of the line and *Spot* on the right, and other times reversed (see Figure 3 for these examples). In this way the teacher combines a tracking activity with word identification, and has a record of how well the learner can discriminate between two familiar words.

Just as adults or older learners may want to create their own key word cards, they may also want to create their own tracking exercises by combining the writing of braille with creating these exercises. It is extremely important that learners first understand that after they have created the tracking exercises, they must be sure to keep their fingers moving over the characters and words in order to prevent scrubbing. They should have little difficulty doing this since they created the exercises themselves and will not be tempted to stop to identify the words. Teachers can then develop similar but different tracking activities for testing purposes—to be sure that the individuals have not learned the words by position on the line or page.

As indicated earlier, the steps of this approach to learning to read can occur simultaneously. While learners are practicing the tracking exercises, the teacher can also introduce new key words to the learner using the method already described. As new words are learned, they are added to

FIGURE 3: Jean and Spot Take a Walk

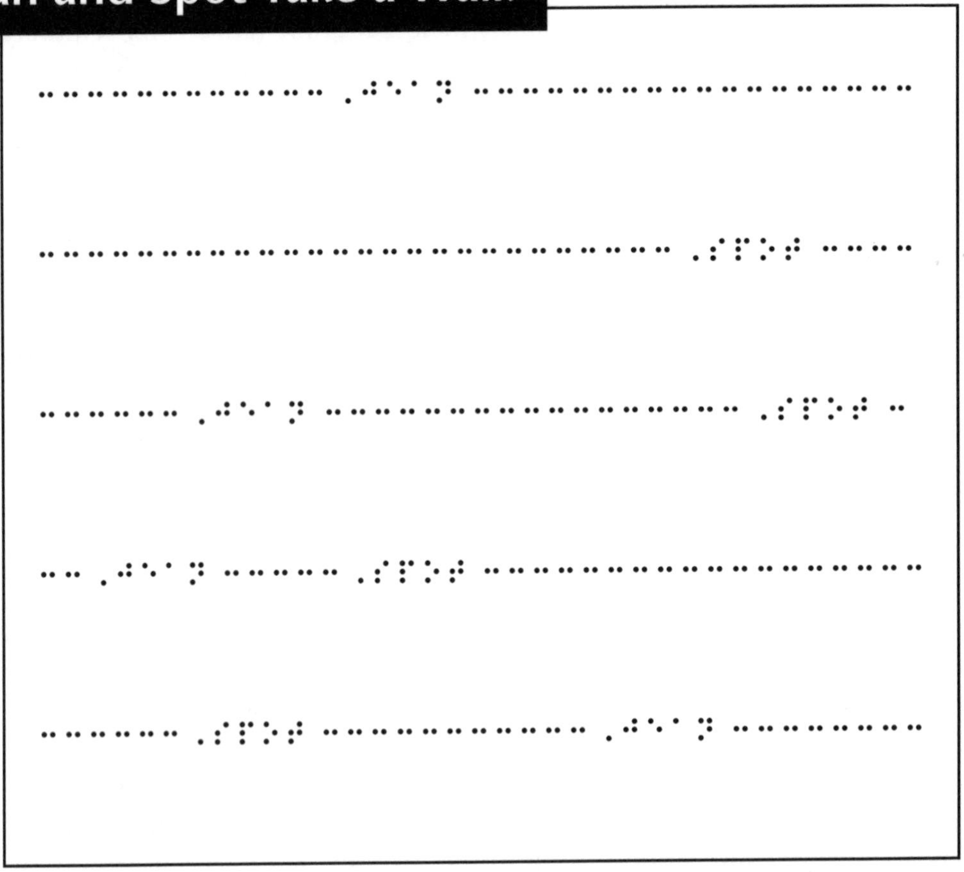

the word box. They are then added to the discrimination games and used in new scenarios for tracking. At the same time, the teacher can begin to introduce identification of letters.

IDENTIFYING LETTERS

When the learner can track lines of braille that contain at least two key words, and can recognize these words when they occur, it is time to work on identifying letters. The learner may wish to make a letter box for letters and decorate it in the same way as the word box. The teacher might want to select the most tactilely distinct first letter of one of the key words as the first letter to identify. The letter should be chosen carefully, since building success in recognition of letters is important. For this first letter, pick the one that has the fewest dots and, if possible, stay away from letters that tactile readers typically confuse (such as *i* and *e,* or *f, d, h,* and *j*).

Introduce this letter in the same manner that the first key word was introduced, using flash cards with lead-in lines. When introducing the letter, relate it to the key word and make the sound that it makes in the key word. For instance, if Sam's key word is *radio,* then the letter *r* would have the sound /r/, as in *radio.* Swenson (personal communication, May 5, 2003) suggests that this is also a good time to point out distinctive characteristics of a letter that the learner will notice when moving his or her fingers across braille characters. (For example, the letter *y* has a big hole on the left and the letter *r* has a hole on the top and bottom right). Initially, create lines of *r*'s to track and throw in the word *radio* as a check to be sure that the learner is really paying attention to what he or she is feeling, and not just tracking the lines. Active participation in tracking wherein the learner is constantly evaluating what is under the fingertips is essential.

Ask the learner to provide other words that begin with the /r/ sound; at the same time, examine the vocabulary words collected previously for any other words beginning with /r/. If the learner doesn't suggest these words, the teacher may suggest them. This can be a good time to introduce another /r/ word, because the beginning letter will be the same and this exercise can begin to teach the discrimination of words that begin with the same letter.

The /r/ sound flash cards can be used in the same games that were previously used for words. Having several cards with *r* on them, as well as multiple sets of cards for the key words learned to this point, allows for many different sorting games. Some examples of sorting games include:

- Find every card that has the word *Sam* on it.

- Find every card that has only an *r* on it.

- Find every card that has the word *radio* on it or that has the word *ring* on it, if that is the other word beginning with *r.*

- Find all the words beginning with *r* and then make piles of cards containing *radio* and *ring.*

As when teaching key words and tracking, the teacher needs to be creative to devise motivating and fun activities and games that provide practice reading these letters and increase the accuracy and recognition skills of the learners, no matter what their age.

For children, introducing each letter one at a time will promote successful recognition, and the order in which they are presented may be related primarily to the beginning letters of the learner's key words to make the exercise as meaningful as possible. By contrast, adults, who may already have learned to read, are likely to be anxious to learn the new code. Adults may begin to move ahead more quickly at this point and may want to begin to practice letter identification of the entire alphabet. Be sure to continue to add words for each letter. An example of a letter identification page for adults might have one character that is different from all the other characters in each row, and they must find the different one. At this point in the letter identification phase for adults, the Mangold materials (Mangold, 1989) may be used sucessfully without modification.

As each new letter is introduced, the teacher needs to create activities and games that discriminate it from the other letters. There are several ways to do this:

- Create a tracking sheet on which there are complete lines repeating only one letter with a space on either side of it, and have the learner indicate what letter it is. The space on either side is helpful initially because it separates the letters and allows the learner to feel each letter separately, in addition to feeling an entire line of the letter. The repetition of the pattern of the dots moving underneath the fingers helps with identification.

- Develop a tracking activity sheet on which the same letter repeats five or six times in a row and then switches to another letter that has been learned. Vary the number of times each letter appears so that the learner does not begin to anticipate when the letter will switch. This activity can take up an entire page, double- or triple-spaced depending on the learner.

- Create a tracking sheet on which a line begins with one letter, and then within the line, a few different letters are "hiding," and ask the learner to tell you when he or she finds them.

As with every aspect of the program, the teacher needs to continue to create more and more activities and games to help the learner become accurate in recognizing the letters.

STEP 6

Assessing Phonemic Awareness

Another important component of any literacy program is the assessment of phonemic awareness. *Phonemic awareness* is "the ability to hear and manipulate the sounds in spoken words and the understanding that spoken words and syllables are made up of sequences of speech sounds" (Yopp, 1992). While some may think that assessment and instruction in phonemic awareness must precede the steps that have already been described, on the contrary, it is precisely because these learners are not traditional learners and require an alternative approach, that the steps in assessing and instructing in phonemic awareness must be based on the key words that are meaningful to the learner. These are typically learners for whom the world is a confusing place. The more the teacher can integrate what is meaningful to the learner into instruction, the more likely it is that he or she will be able to succeed in learning to read. Research suggests that phonemic awareness grows with increased exposure to reading tasks and with actual engagement with reading materials (Moustafa, 1995).

Learners who lack phonemic awareness skills may have difficulty in any or all of the following phonemic awareness skill areas: grouping words with similar and dissimilar sounds (e.g., *rat, rug, sun*); blending and splitting syllables into onset and rime (the beginning consonant and the ending sound, as in b-eet), blending sounds into words (/s/-/u/-/n/); segmenting a word as a sequence of distinct sounds, or phonemes (e.g., *ship* is made up of three phonemes, /sh/, /i/, /p/); or detecting and manipulating sounds within words (e.g., changing *r* in run to *s* to make *sun*) (Kame'enui et al., 1997).

There are two instruments that would be good starting places for the assessment of phonemic awareness. The first is the Dynamic Indicators of Basic Early Literacy Skills or DIBELS (2002) assessment of phonemic awareness. The drawback to this instrument is that it is based heavily on the use of pictures. For learners who are visually impaired, it is possible to do the assessment using objects. For example, a real feather can be substituted for the picture of a feather. Time is required to collect the types of objects necessary for this assessment and to ensure that these objects have meaning to the learner. If the learner does not know the names of the objects, the assessment will not provide a useful picture of the learner's phonemic awareness capabilities.

Another instrument is the Texas Primary Reading Inventory (2003). This instrument does not rely heavily on pictures and thus is more readily adaptable for learners who are visually impaired.

Learners who were fluent readers prior to their vision loss will have mastered the various aspects of phonemic awareness including detecting rhymes, counting syllables, matching initial sounds, counting phonemes, comparing word length, and representing phonemes with letters. Rehabilitation teachers who work with adults and teachers of visually impaired student who work with teenagers should obtain information about the types of reading activities the learners performed independently prior to losing their vision. This information will help teachers determine whether or not to use a test to assess a learner's phonemic awareness skills. However, phonemic awareness assessment will always be necessary with younger children and possibly with learners who speak English as a second language who may not be familiar with the phonemes in English.

Once the learner's level of phonemic awareness is identified, the activities suggested in the next section to teach phonemic awareness and phonics can be incorporated into the functional approach already underway.

STEP 7

Teaching Phonemic Awareness and Phonics

Phonics is the relationship between sounds and the symbols that represent them. Readers must be able to translate from the symbol to the sound; writers must be able to translate from the sound to the symbol. The teaching of phonics usually addresses both and often incorporates spelling as part of the phonics program. Phonemic awareness instruction has been found to be more effective when paired with phonics instruction—wherein students can manipulate written symbols to see how the sounds change when phonemes are interchanged, especially when the words are used in context (Moustafa, 1995)—for example, changing the medial vowel in *p-d* from *pad* to *ped* to *pod* to *pud* to *pid* to see what happens to the sound of the word.

Some research studies suggest that systematic and explicit phonics instruction is more effective than nonsystematic instruction or no phonics instruction (Alder, 2001). The larger issue, however, is not whether phonics should be taught but whether it should be taught in the traditional way, with worksheets and drill, or within a more meaningful context (F.M. D'Andrea, personal communication, June 6, 2003). Moreover, most research studies on reading skills include only children who are sighted. The subjects of these studies would have had unlimited access to the words and symbols of their reading medium, unlike most braille readers, and the activity of reading itself would almost certainly have been meaningful to these typical learners. By contrast, many of the learners for whom the functional braille literacy approach will be useful have had limited contact with braille texts. It is therefore especially important that explicit instruction in phonics is presented in a meaningful context for these students. The key word vocabulary is once again central in achieving this. These words provide the basis for the symbols that will be used in explicit phonics instruction, and as more and more key words are learned, there will be more and more opportunities for providing phonics instruction from the units that make up those words. Support for this approach can be found in the research on print reading done by Vellutin and Scanlon (1987).

There are many ways to use the key word vocabulary to teach phonics to those learners who have not already learned to read print. The following are some suggestions on how to incorporate meaningful vocabulary with phonics instruction:

1. Use the beginning consonants from the key words and create books of words beginning with the same symbol or sound. For example, if a learner's key word is *bad,* other words that start with the same

letter can be introduced, such as *book, balloon, backpack, banana, bee, bow,* and so on. The teacher can make a page of the book for each word and try to find items that are small enough in size to be physically attached to the pages in some way. *Balloon* is a perfect example since a balloon (not blown up) or a bag of balloons can easily be attached to the page. The words *balloon* and *bag of balloons* should be brailled on the pages to which they are attached. For the word *book,* the teacher can attach a miniature book such as the kind that is generally available in bookstores. (The teacher might even be able to put some braille on the pages of this little book.) The word books that the teacher creates should be made of sturdy material since learners will want to take them back and forth from school to home and read them to others. For an older student, this activity can be made more age-appropriate if the learner feels that the book is being created for a younger learner with whom it will be shared. This book-making activity is critical to the student's understanding of what reading and phonics are all about and is a transition to a much broader literacy experience. Making these books *with* a child rather than *for* a child helps the student to develop important concepts about how books are put together (A. Swenson, May 5, 2003).

2. Examine the key words for patterns and present other words in which these same patterns occur. This is often referred to as "onset/rime" where, as noted earlier, the beginning consonant is the *onset* and the ending of the word is the *rime.* Onset/rime instruction has been found to be a powerful way to introduce phonics skills (Moustafa, 1995). For example, if the key word is *bad,* other words that could be introduced are *dad, mad, sad, pad, glad,* and so on. The teacher can create word cards for these words, and they can be included in the Word Box when the learner can read them. Have the student practice writing these words (see Step 8) and using them in stories (see Step 10).

3. Examine the key words for consonant blends.
   Example: Key word: *Brittany* (name of friend)
   Other words: *bring, bread, brown*

4. Examine the key words for vowel patterns.
Example: Key word: *beat*
Other words: *heat, neat, seat, treat, meat, eat*

5. Examine the key words for any other patterns that can lead to other words with similar patterns.

There are many books available that provide teachers with words containing blends, digraphs, and vowel patterns. A great resource for this is Miller (2001), *The Reading Teacher's Survival Kit*. Some beginning spelling books work well for this. When choosing the other words, the teacher should determine whether the words have meaning for the learner; if they do not, then the teacher must develop ways to make the words meaningful. For instance, *feat* has the same vowel pattern as *beat* in the example above but it would be important to determine whether the learner has ever heard the word used, and if not, to provide the learner with examples of usage. In addition, introducing a word such as *feat* would provide the basis for discussing homonyms and introducing the word *feet*, which should be meaningful to the learner. These words feel different, especially if the *ea* sign is used in *feat*. However, the teacher would need to know whether the learner is ready for homonyms or whether this new information would be too confusing.

Used in this way, the key words become building blocks for introducing more and more meaningful vocabulary words that learners can read. At the same time, the key words are also providing the learner with knowledge that enhances phonemic awareness and phonics skills.

STEP 8

Developing Mechanics and Process: Writing Skills

The literacy activities described up to this point all have to do with reading. As these activities are being introduced, the learner should also be developing writing skills. Initially, teacher and learner will be mainly concentrating on the mechanics of writing rather than on the creative process. The lessons that stress mechanics will also incorporate reading the letters and key words that the student has already learned.

As the learner begins to identify individual letters, the teacher can demonstrate how to form these letters using the Perkins brailler. At some point, learners may also be introduced to the slate and stylus. Initially, however, the brailler is preferable because it provides the learner with immediate feedback as to what was written and also provides a necessary cognitive link between reading and writing. Writing can be integrated with reading in a variety of ways depending upon the ability of the learner. The main thing to keep in mind is that for these learners, the writing instruction needs to be derived from the key words and the sounds being learned.

TEACHING THE BRAILLEWRITER

To become an independent user of the Perkins brailler, the learner will need to be able to locate the paper, position the braillewriter on the work surface, put the paper in the brailler, roll it back in the braillewriter, lock in the paper, and move the carriage return to the beginning of the line to begin writing. The learner will also need to use the line spacing key to move from one line to the next. Depending on the learner's capabilities, the teacher may want to introduce the tasks using backward chaining, which involves starting with the last step of a task, and teaching that step first, so that the learner can have immediate success. Once the learner masters the last step, the step immediately preceding it is taught, and so on, until the entire task is learned. For example, to teach how to put paper in the brailler, the teacher might have the learner start with the paper already in the brailler and have the student learn to hit the line spacing key prior to actually writing symbols. The teacher can use a checklist such as the one in Figure 4, to keep track of the various mechanical aspects of writing that the learner has mastered.

To introduce the way that letters are formed on the Perkins brailler, teachers can use enlarged braille cells of various types. A Swing Cell, available from American Printing House for the Blind, resembles a large braille cell with six holes into which pegs can be placed to represent the dots of the braille cell. The two sides of the enlarged cell are hinged and can swing

FIGURE 4: Sample Form for Recording Students' Progress in Learning to Use a Brailler

MECHANICS OF USING A BRAILLER
Assessment and Sequence of Skills

Recording Procedures: I = Skill introduced
A = Skill achieved with assistance
M = Skill achieved with mastery

Skills	I	A	M
1. Identifies and uses the following parts of the brailler:			
embossing bar			
spacing keys			
backspacing key			
paper release levers			
paper feed knob			
embossing head lever			
line spacing key			
support bar			
feed roller			
left paper stop			
warning bell			
handle			
cover			
margin stop			
2. Operates brailler:			
Positions brailler correctly on work surface.			
Moves embossing head to correct positions.			
Rotates paper feed knob away from self.			
Pulls paper release levers all the way toward self.			
Holds paper against paper support with one hand and closes paper release with the other.			
Rolls paper into brailler until stopped by left paper stop.			
Depresses the line spacing key to lock paper position.			
Removes paper from the brailler.			
Leaves brailler in rest position when not in use (moves embossing head to the right as far as possible, leaves paper release lever open, and covers machine).			

Source: Adapted from Rosemary Swallow, Sally S. Mangold, and Philip Mangold, Eds., *Informal Assessment of Developmental Skills for Visually Handicapped Students* (New York: American Foundation for the Blind, 1978).

A Swing Cell with the letter "t" formed as it looks when being read.

open. When closed, the dots formed by the pegs resemble the character created by brailling. When opened, the cell corresponds to the keys of the Perkins brailler. Using this device, the teacher can help the student place the correct pegs in the Swing Cell to represent a particular braille character. Then the teacher can help the learner place the appropriate fingers on the "dots" in the Swing Cell to learn correct finger placement for writing that character on the brailler. The learner then transfers these fingers to the appropriate keys of the Perkins brailler. From this experience, the learner can discover which fingers are needed to create a letter using the keys on the Perkins. In addition, using the Swing Cell reinforces the dot formation of the letter that the learner is already reading.

One caution when using enlarged braille cell simulations is to avoid an overreliance on them. As long as learners are working with enlarged materials, they are not reading regular braille. Although it might initially

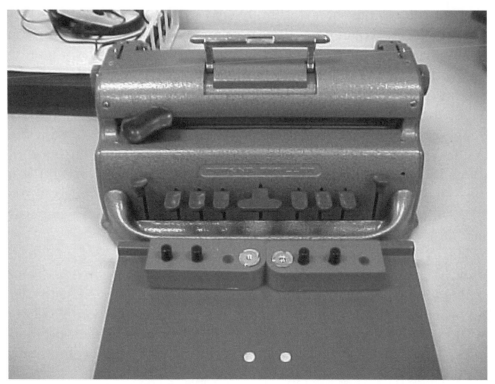

The Swing Cell opened up so that the holes match the keys on the Perkins brailler. The pegs forming the letter "t" now show where the student's fingers should be placed on the keys for brailling.

seem easier to use enlarged cell formats to teach braille symbol configurations, enlarged cells should not be used for reading unless the learner has severe tactile discrimination impairments that preclude the use of regular paper braille. In fact, Pester, Petrosko, and Poppe (1994) found that standard braille proved to be significantly faster for subjects to discriminate as opposed to enlarged braille. Learners need to learn to read regular paper braille.

TEACHING THE SLATE AND STYLUS

For those learners who will learn to use the slate and stylus, the teacher may want to refer to the dot positions in the cell either by number or by position. The dot numbers refer to the positions of the dots in the cell.

The first column has three dots numbered 1 through 3 from top to bottom. The second column has three dots numbered 4 through 6 from top to bottom. Once the dot numbers in a character are learned for writing on the braillewriter, the formation of the character on the slate can be referred to in the same manner. By using either number positions, or spatial positions of the dots within the cell as a referent, teachers do not have to ask learners to "reverse" what they have learned in writing on the braillewriter to writing on the slate. They only reverse the direction in which they write. On the braillewriter, they write from left to right. On the slate, they write from right to left. The first column on the braillewriter is on the left side; the first column on the slate is on the right side. Otherwise, the dot positions remain the same.

Thus, when a learner forms the braille character *t*, dots 2-3-4-5 are used. Dots 2-3 are in the first column of the cell and dots 4-5 are in the second column of the cell. On the slate, these same dots are depressed, with dots 2-3 being in the first column working from the right, and dots 4-5 being in the second column. If the learner refers to the dots by their position within the cell, he or she may talk about a dot in the first column top position, or second column middle or bottom positions.

⠞   equals *t* on the braillewriter

⠻   equals *t* on the slate

In addition to working with the individual letters already learned, the teacher needs to institute fingering activities on the Perkins brailler to develop learners' finger strength and dexterity. Learners with weak fingers need strength-building games developed for them. For example, creating a braille wave (Simons, 1997), by pressing dots 1, 2, 3, 4, 5, 6 in order, is a good activity to teach separate use of the fingers. Learners can also press various keys at the same time to make tracking patterns to follow (full cell, top dots, middle dots, bottom dots, etc.) and can also make up tracking sheets for letter recognition. This reinforces the letters learned and allows the learner to create his or her own "reading material." Each line to track could consist of one item initially, for example a whole line of full cells (separated by spaces), or a whole line of dots 1 and 4, or 2 and

5, or 3 and 6 for example. Learners should double- or triple-space the lines on these sheets initially.

When introducing the writing of letters, the teacher should also reinforce the letter sounds by having the learner say the sound of the letter when writing it. The teacher can ask the student to name other words starting with that sound, as in the activities described in Step 7. Use the first key word and teach the learner to write all the letters in that word. Depending on the length of the word, this will provide a set of letters to be written, and the learner can simultaneously work on reading these letters in the tracking exercises. The learner's input in creating tracking activities will make the exercise twice as meaningful (functional).

Older children and adults may take readily to this step as it is generally easier to learn to use the writing tools than it is to develop the tactile perception necessary to read the braille, so it gives them instant success as a student and can motivate them to continue to work on developing their tactile perceptual skills. And, as was mentioned earlier, incorporating writing with reading can be helpful in developing tactile perception.

STEP 9

Creating Functional Uses for Reading and Writing

All the steps discussed so far will be repeated over and over again for a learner as new key words and new words from various phonics lessons are introduced, learned, and stored in the word box. The teacher will also want to introduce words that are functional for the learners, even if the learners themselves have not suggested these words. For example, the

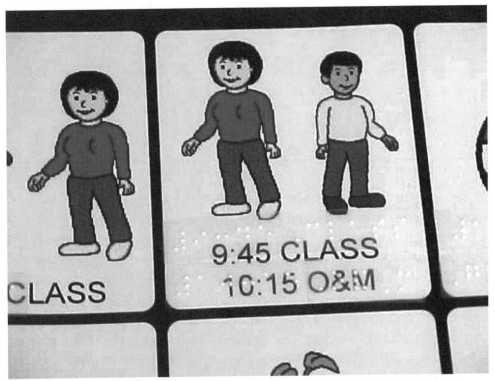

Part of a student's schedule for the day, shown in print, braille, and picture symbols. Reading the schedule is a functional literacy activity that also helps build vocabulary.

daily or weekly schedule of activities can be brailled and words from that schedule can be incorporated into the learner's reading and writing vocabulary. Reading this schedule on a regular basis is a functional literacy activity that can be purposeful for all types of learners. These words will contain new letters and phonics patterns to be learned and thus contribute to building the learner's repertoire of recognizable vocabulary words.

Labeling items in the environment is another way to make reading functional for the learner, as discussed earlier. In addition to reading the labels, it is possible to have the learner create the labels once he or she can write the letters of the words. Labeling can expand into many avenues beyond simply labeling items with the user's name. Items of clothing can be labeled with their colors, as can the settings on the microwave (such as for popcorn or defrosting frozen food). Learners can also label spices, commonly used tools, cassette tapes or CDs, and anything else the learner wants to identify.

Reading simple recipes and using them to make snacks or quick meals is another way to expand the functional reading and writing vocabulary. Grocery lists can be created for the recipes, and more new words can be added from the foods that the learner enjoys. The teacher needs to be constantly on the alert for more functional uses of reading and writing braille to expand the learner's literacy base.

Adult learners respond very positively to this step in the approach, as using braille in truly functional ways helps them gain back some of the independence that they may have lost as a result of their visual impairment. It may also be the step that convinces them to continue learning braille and to try to learn to use braille to read short passages or familiar stories.

STEP 10

Creating Stories

At the same time that the functional uses of braille are being expanded, the learner may have acquired enough vocabulary words to create stories using these words. The stories may also serve to further expand the learner's reading and writing vocabulary. Initially stories should be meaningful and fun for learners, whatever their age. The following are some guidelines for helping learners develop their initial stories:

1. Use repetition in the stories to facilitate reading. Either the key phrase can be repeated or one word can be repeated. An example might be the following story:

    Jim and Hannah

    Jim and Hannah ate breakfast.

    Jim and Hannah ate a snack.

    Jim and Hannah ate lunch.

Jim and Hannah ate another snack.

Jim and Hannah ate dinner.

Jim and Hannah are not hungry anymore!

2. Repeat new words in stories to increase fluency with these words. In the following example, the student had just learned the word *rigatoni,* which was his favorite food.

<u>We All Ate Rigatoni</u>

Jim ate rigatoni.

Maria ate rigatoni.

Sam ate rigatoni.

Mrs. B. ate rigatoni.

Tony ate rigatoni.

We all ate rigatoni.

And, boy, did we like it!

3. Make the sentences short initially and then gradually expand the length.

4. Triple-space stories initially, and then decrease to double-spacing as readers become more capable.

5. Keep the stories that have been created for and by learners in a note-book, which they can decorate themselves if they wish.

6. Have learners try to create stories that resemble those in the Dr. Seuss books. These stories use many rhyming words and repeated patterns. Depending on the types of phonics activities that the learners have been introduced to, these books also may be suitable for use with the learner.

Reading and rereading stories that are familiar can help promote the development of fluency in reading. Rereading helps to develop efficient tracking skills, eliminate scrubbing, and promote automatic word recognition. In addition, fluency is highly correlated with reading comprehension (A. Swenson, May 5, 2003).

Adults who have already learned to read can read stories they are most familiar with to help them become accustomed to the "feel" of reading braille. The rehabilitation teacher can ask the learner what stories or nursery rhymes he or she remembers reading as a child. Reading these familiar stories, such as Humpty Dumpty or Little Miss Muffett, can be a way to introduce contractions and short-form words, to allow for prediction and anticipation, and to permit the learner to have success in reading. Or, learners may wish to create sentences to practice using some of their favorite key words. These can be brailled onto cards for use with the magnetic card reader so that learners can check for accuracy. The way in which the rehabilitation teacher builds story reading into the approach will depend very much on the desires of the adult learner. The rehabilitation teacher needs to probe to find out what reading materials might be suitable for each individual client.

STEP 11

Record Keeping and Diagnostic Teaching

The functional approach is an individualized and personalized approach. This makes it extremely important for the teacher to keep accurate and detailed records of what each learner has accomplished. The teacher must continually assess what problems students are having and develop techniques or materials to assist students in overcoming problems or hurdles as they emerge. This is referred to as *diagnostic teaching,* a form of ongoing assessment and remediation of problems that students have, and is a critical piece of the functional approach. Teachers cannot wait for a formal reading assessment to discover a student's particular weaknesses or difficulties. They must address the difficulties as they occur and remediate them while continuing to move forward with instruction.

The list of key vocabulary words from the teacher's initial assessment must be readily available at all times. Since vocabulary that is meaningful and functional for the learner is the basis for instruction, teachers will refer back to this list frequently when designing instruction. As the learner begins to be able to read the key words, these need to be entered into the learner's records. Having a list of the key words that are in the word box as a reference will also assist the teacher in developing subsequent learning activities for both reading and writing. Figure 5 shows an example of a chart that can be used for recording the learner's key word vocabulary.

It is not enough for the teacher to use diagnostic teaching to remediate a problem. Teachers must also keep records of the particular types of problems learners have with recognizing words or characters, the activities that were developed to remediate these problems, and the results of the remediation. Samples of tracking exercises that were particularly successful should also be kept in the learner's file for future reference. These exercises may need to be repeated with new characters or words as the student continues to learn. Some words may initally be too difficult for the learner. The teacher may wish to put these words aside (into a pocket in the file, for example) to try again later when the learner has had a little more tactile experience with reading.

Additional items that are useful to keep track of include:

- letters that the student learns to identify and to write

- contractions that the student learns to identify and to write

- phonics patterns that the student has mastered in reading

- activities that the student particularly likes (These can be motivating escapes from more difficult work.)

- stories that have been written and which ones the student enjoyed most

Record keeping helps with designing future instruction and in determining if, when, and how to move into a more traditional approach to learning to read and write.

Sample Form for Recording Vocabulary Words

KEY WORD VOCABULARY

Word	Date Introduced	Dates of Practice	Date Mastered

When to Move into a More Traditional Academic Approach

Since the functional braille literacy approach is built around only the words that are in the experience of the learner, it has certain built-in limitations similar to those of the language experience approach. However, there are elements of the functional approach that can be adapted to almost any reading program. At some point, if the student is making good progress in learning to read and write, the teacher may wish him or her to make the transition into a more traditional academic approach or a modified academic approach to learning to read and write. Many times teachers want their students to begin using a basal reading series, such as the *Patterns* series (Caton, Pester, & Bradley, 1980), which was developed especially for braille readers, or another commercially available reading series. But learners who have been using an approach geared to their own interests may not be as motivated by approaches based on more traditional basal readers.

There are many simple yet motivating books available for sighted beginning readers. These books are leveled (in other words they are designed for various grade levels of reading), and many can be enjoyed without the pictures. They can be adapted for braille readers by brailling the text on clear braille labels and attaching these to the pages. Students' motivation can be maintained as they make the transition to a more traditional approach if books from this group are selected to meet both their learning needs and interests. Regular classroom teachers usually don't mind if teachers of students who are visually impaired borrow these books from this group and adapt them (A. Swenson, May 5, 2003).

Adult learners in particular, may want to move into reading stories and literature centered around a theme that interests them. Or an older reader may be ready to move into a series specifically designed for older learners, such as *Braille Too* (Hepker & Coquillette, 1995) or *The Braille Connection* (Caton, Gordon, Pesler, Roderick, & Modaressi, 1997).

In general, let the learner's strengths and the volume of what he or she has learned be the guide as to what type of approach to lead into. For example, a learner who knows almost all the letters of the alphabet and is capable of recognizing them and has some basic reading vocabulary might be ready to move into a variety of approaches. For guidance in determining whether or not to move into a basal reader, a more explicit phonics-based approach, or a literature-based approach, the teacher needs to consider what the learner has enjoyed previously. The teacher may also wish to utilize high-interest low-vocabulary readers to continue to develop reading skills and preteach contractions in the stories to be read (see the Resources section for some sources of these books). The teacher can continue to develop vocabulary using the functional approach. In fact, even when the learner is capable of reading everything in the more traditional approach as it is encountered and taught, the functional approach may still be necessary to ensure that the materials to be read are age-appropriate and relate to what the learner is doing.

In order to determine the type of approach to transition the learner into, it is important that the teacher have a good understanding of the variety of approaches that are used in teaching reading and writing. It is also important to know the formats of the few curriculum materials that are designed for the consistent introduction of contracted braille. These curricula are described in the Appendix of this book.

Summary

The functional braille literacy program will facilitate the development of reading and writing skills by a variety of learners who have difficulty learning with more traditional methods by making reading and writing a meaningful and pleasurable activity. Teachers should not expect that miracles will occur overnight, however, and will need to constantly and consistently work with their students to ensure that they succeed to the best of their abilities. Accurate and complete records of student progress need to be kept. The learning process may take place over several years and will be highly individualized. A student's future teachers will appreciate accurate and thorough record keeping so they can continue to present and build on the type of instruction that has proven successful for that learner.

In Part 2, a series of case studies illustrates how the steps that have been discussed in this section are applied with different kinds of learners. These examples demonstrate how the functional braille literacy approach is individualized according to the specific needs of the learner.

Using the Functional Braille Literacy Approach with Different Kinds of Learners

Although the steps of the functional braille literacy approach to teaching reading and writing remain essentially the same for all learners, there are modifications that must be made for learners with different needs to permit them to benefit from the program and become literate to the best of their abilities. This section provides descriptions of individuals from the different groups of learners who tend to have difficulty with traditional teaching methods and benefit from the functional braille literacy approach: children with visual impairments who have additional disabilities, including various degrees of cognitive impairments, physical disabilities, and deaf-blindness, and older children and adults who may or may not have learned to read print, and who may be coping with the onset of adventitious blindness or with learning English as a second language. These case studies provide examples of ways that teachers can implement the functional braille literacy approach with different types of learners as well as incorporate the specific needs of each individual.

Learners with Mild to Moderate Cognitive Impairments:

BRIANNA

Brianna is 19 years old and is now reading material at first- and second-grade level. She is legally blind (light perception only), and in a life skills program with several other learners her own age who are visually impaired and who also have mild to moderate cognitive impairment. She has a pleasant personality and is always eager to show others what she can do. She enjoys singing in her church choir and in the school chorus.

At 15, Brianna was able to write the first ten letters of the alphabet, but was unable to read them consistently. Brianna's listening comprehension, measured using an informal reading inventory, placed her at the pre-primer or primer level. She had many gaps in understanding of the material read. Her teacher began working with her and her classmates using a functional approach to learning braille. She and her classmates created stories about themselves and put all of the stories they wrote into story books, which they decorated. Reading their stories together always provided a great deal of enjoyment and laughter.

Brianna had always been a compliant learner who did whatever her teachers asked. However, from the beginning of the use of the functional approach, Brianna became much more involved and excited about her reading. Brianna selected her own reading vocabulary using her word box, and loved to use the talking card reader to check her own reading. Her teacher instituted the use of the *Mangold Developmental Program of Tactile Perception and Braille Letter Recognition* with Brianna. Her recognition of letters improved as she also began to be able to recognize letters in the words from her word box. Brianna needed a great deal of work on vocabulary, since her experiences were limited. The songs that Brianna loved and had memorized were transcribed into braille for her to practice reading. She practiced reading stories at the preprimer level and then read them to younger preschool children. This was very motivating to her, since she loved being around the younger children and they loved having her read to them.

Her teacher began moving Brianna into a more modified academic approach when they finished the Mangold program. At that time, Brianna could recognize all the letters consistently, and had over 100 words in her word box. In addition, she was reading the stories the class had created without prompting, and appeared to be recognizing the words as well as having memorized the stories. Her teacher had also been using the Dolch word list (also called sight words, these are the most frequently used words for various age groups) with Brianna, especially the nouns and verbs, for vocabulary development and for practice in reading. They often used these words to write sentences on talking card reader cards that Brianna would then read independently and check using the machine.

Now at 19, Brianna is reading contracted braille and knows almost all of the contractions and short-form words. Her reading comprehension is still at an elementary school grade level, but she is able to make her own grocery lists, and read menus, write letters to her friends and is much more involved in her own education. She uses a braille notetaker with speech for keeping files, including her songs and her recipes. She has also begun writing her own stories using her braille notetaker. Just how much of an academic literacy program Brianna will be able to master before she reaches the mandatory graduation age of 21 is still unknown. However, her teachers feel that the functional approach is what enabled her to make such good progress in reading over the past four years.

The functional braille literacy approach was really designed with learners like Brianna in mind. Learners with mild to moderate cognitive impairments will generally be able to achieve some degree of literacy and may even be candidates for a modified basic literacy approach if they demonstrate a level of capability similar to Brianna's. Once learners recognize that reading has meaning for them, they get excited about reading and begin to blossom, as Brianna did. Many of these individuals have scattered skills, but with the functional approach, they may demonstrate mastery of some of the skills or tasks that could eventually lead them into a more conventional literacy program. Using a functional approach with these learners helps to determine where their gaps are and addresses those gaps within a context that is meaningful for them.

A braille-rich environment is important for all learners, and this group is no exception. Teachers need to repeatedly expose the learners to the braille words in their environment and to tell them what the words mean. For example, a teacher might say, "Here is your name on your locker. Here is Jessie's name. Here is the word that means 'on' on the light switch, and here is the word that means 'off.'" Teachers do this over and over with the print words in the environment for typically sighted children who are mildly to moderately cognitively impaired. Providing the same type of exposure for learners who are blind or visually impaired fosters the expectation that perhaps someday these learners will demonstrate an understanding of what reading is and what letters and words are.

The functional approach can be initiated at any age with this population. The steps listed in Part 1 require little or no modification. By giving learners like Brianna a more meaningful approach to learning to read, the hope is that they will be able to make more progress earlier on. However, teachers may find that these learners continue to remain in the emergent literacy stage for an extended period of time, and require many more concrete learning activities and experiences to develop the language experience base that other children may gain more quickly. The key is to not give up on these learners. Had Brianna's teachers decided early in her education that she simply was not going to make any progress in braille reading and switched to teaching her using a solely auditory mode of communication, Brianna would not have the literacy skills that she has today.

Learners with mild to moderate cognitive disabilities may also have difficulty expressing themselves—and may not be able to select words by themselves for their key word vocabulary. The teacher may need to prompt them for words collected in the initial assessment and help them realize that they have things going on in their lives that are very exciting to them and about which they might want to learn to read. For example, Brianna loved to sing and was able to memorize all the songs for her church choir and the school chorus. Having the words for her favorite songs in braille was exciting to her.

Brianna's teacher made her favorite songs into storybooks with one line per page. Since Brianna already knew the words by heart, and knew where to pause at the end of each line, she had a better idea of what words were on each line. She and her teacher could talk about how to recognize words on the line that were tactilely distinct. The teacher used uncontracted braille, which she felt better lent itself to this approach since Brianna could feel the spaces between every word.

As Brianna began to learn contracted braille, her teacher was able to take the words she had learned in uncontracted braille from the songs and show Brianna what they would look like in contracted braille. She would write the words on cards for Brianna to put in her word box, with the contracted braille on one side of the card and the uncontracted braille on the other, so Brianna could test herself. For some reason, Brianna really delighted in this activity, and found the switch to contracted braille humorous. Every time the teacher would show her another word that could now be written a different way—a shorter way—Brianna would say, "Oh, no, not another one!" and then laugh out loud. This phrase, of course, also made its way into the word box!

There may also be a greater need for concentrated phonemic awareness activities for children with mild or moderate cognitive impairment than for the general population of children who are blind or visually impaired. They are not as adept at puzzling out the sounds in their environment. An assessment of the learner's level of phonemic awareness gives the teacher a starting point from which to introduce appropriate games and activities that can increase phonemic awareness capabilities. Increasing these capabilities is a very important part of this approach to reading and writing with these learners.

Learners in this group often love writing even more than they do reading. It seems to be easier for them to learn the mechanics of pressing down the keys on the brailler than it is to learn to recognize the characters they produce. The important thing to remember is that the writing must be as meaningful as the reading. Teachers should help learners create for themselves some of the same materials they will be learning to read. This helps them understand the relationship between reading and writing.

When learners are creating stories, teachers may need to prompt them to use their key words. Learners need to be made to feel that what they have to say is important enough to write down and read, and to include in a booklet for reading and rereading.

With learners such as Brianna, as with all learners for whom a functional approach is being used, it is particularly important for the teacher to be alert for signs of when a learner has really begun to catch on to reading and when they are ready to move into a more traditional approach. Teachers should expect this to happen. Ask when a learner will be ready to move on, not if. Generally, when the student has learned all or almost all of the letters of the alphabet, has a good grasp of phonics, and has a word box (or two or three) that is full to overflowing with words that he or she can read, it is time to move on into more formal reading materials.

The materials to use with such a reader need to be exciting and motivating, as the initial foray into a more traditional approach will occur rather slowly. The teacher should introduce any new vocabulary words in a story, explain new concepts, and possibly create experiences for learners to help them develop those concepts. As an example, the girls in Brianna's class were reading a story about a teenager who wanted to get her nails done. The girls had many questions about this and to help answer their questions, their teacher took the girls to a local nail salon. Each girl had her nails done, and while they were there, Brianna's teacher emphasized words like "nail polish," "salon," "cuticle," "file," "buffer," and "acetate" (because the girls were commenting about the smell of the salon). She also discussed "tips" with them ahead of time—both the tips that they would put on their nails and also what tip they would give to the stylists after their nails were done. After returning to the classroom, one of the girls wanted to know what a French manicure was: she had heard another patron asking for it. Brianna's teacher created a raised-line drawing of a nail with a French manicure for the girls to feel.

One of the greatest challenges of this approach is that reading materials may need to be on a first- or second-grade level and thus may be devoid of real emotion or interest for the student. Teachers need to locate materials that will be interesting for the learner; they may even have to write their own stories. Warner (1963), mentioned in the Introduction, found this to be necessary with her Maori students. Available materials dealt with experiences that were so foreign to her students that they could not relate to them.

Formatting reading material is also important. Stories may have to be prepared in double-spaced braille if the learner is not yet reading single-spaced material. Practice on new words must include continued emphasis on proper tracking and accuracy in word recognition. Although some learners such as Brianna are generally compliant, learners in general will find it much more fun to practice words from stories they are reading, rather than to practice unrelated lists of words such as the Dolch word list. Keeping them motivated and excited is a must!

Learners with Severe to Profound Cognitive Impairments

MATTHEW

Matthew is 9 years old, and totally blind. He has very little expressive language, but is beginning to be more responsive to the activities in his classroom, a resource room for children like Matthew who have severe cognitive impairments. Until recently, he initiated activity only with prompting from the teacher. He has a calendar system composed of objects representing various activities occurring within the school day and is beginning to use this with prompting. He appears to listen during story-reading activities and enjoys the concrete hands-on activities that his teacher incorporates into the reading of the stories. Recently, the teacher read a story about frogs to the class and brought a frog into the classroom for the students to see. She played a tape of the sounds that frogs make. She let Matthew hold the frog in his hands, and showed him where the frog's home was in the classroom. Matthew was enthralled! He has learned to find his way to the frog's home independently and frequently can be found holding his ear close to the terrarium where the frog lives.

Initially, Matthew's resource room teacher, Ms. Gomez, did not think that Matthew would be a good candidate for any kind of literacy program. She was also concerned about trying to attempt a literacy program with him because she did not know braille. However, Matthew's teacher of visually impaired students created a braille-rich environment for Matthew and helped Ms. Gomez feel comfortable exposing him to the braille in his environment. She also provided Ms. Gomez with a braille labeler and tape, and demonstrated how to use these to label any additional items that Matthew showed an interest in.

Ms. Gomez now thinks that Matthew is beginning to recognize his name on his locker and his belongings. He stops to feel the braille names on the list posted outside his classroom, and his teacher thinks he is aware that they are "words" or "names." Since Matthew enjoyed the frog so much, she decided to put the word *frog* on a word card for Matthew and then put *Matthew* on another card. She also put a label that said *frog* on the frog's home, showed Matthew the label, and told him that it said *frog.* She had Matthew examine the cards while she told him which one said *Matthew* and which one said *frog.* After he had examined them for a while, she indicated to Matthew that if he chose the frog card, he could go pay the frog a visit. Matthew immediately picked out the frog card and took it with him to the frog's home.

These experiences have confirmed Matthew's teacher's belief that he could benefit from more concentrated time for a functional approach to braille literacy. She is planning on increasing her time with Matthew to implement the approach and to help the resource room teacher understand the approach.

Teachers of learners with severe to profound cognitive impairments often have low expectations for their students' acquisition of literacy skills, particularly if the student's vision loss is severe enough to indicate the need to be a braille reader. It is interesting to compare teachers' expectations for learners who have severe disabilities and typical vision with the expectations for learners who have severe disabilities but are blind. Teachers of children with severe cognitive impairments but normal vision will point out signs and words in their environment to the children. They will point out the word *Gymnasium* on the gym door. They will point out teachers' names on their classroom doors and the student's name on lockers and other personal possessions. They will also point out other students' names on bulletin boards and in other locations. They will point out signs for restrooms and stairs, exit signs, McDonald's golden arches, and other signs and symbols that they feel the learner may be able to make use of. They may not expect the learner to remember these words or names, but they continue to point them out, watching and hoping for some indication that the learner is catching on to literacy. With learners who are blind or so severely visually impaired that they are candidates for a braille literacy program, the same effort needs to be made to provide a braille-rich environment and to point out words and names in braille. And, teachers need to have the same expectations: that the learner may someday "catch on" to literacy; and when they do, the teacher needs to be ready to take them even further.

For learners like Matthew, some of the steps in the functional braille literacy approach may need modifications. Selecting the individualized reading and writing vocabulary will be a little more difficult with Matthew than with Brianna, since Matthew has so little expressive language. The interviews with family members, caretakers, and others who know Matthew well will be critical for him.

It is possible that developing a key vocabulary for Matthew may also help with his expressive language. He will be concentrating on just a few words initially, and he may be able to learn to say them or even to sign them, or both. Sometimes, with students who have little expressive language and are so passive, it is difficult to find what motivates them. As is clear from his encounters with the class frog, Matthew has interests and is capable of demonstrating what he is interested in. This is a plus for the teacher who is designing his program because it will make it easier to find activities and words that will motivate him.

Communication is a key to literacy with learners such as Matthew. Teachers, families, and early intervention specialists often begin establishing communication by using symbol systems, such as calendar boxes or daily schedules using objects. The teacher starts by helping the child begin to associate an activity with a specific object that has meaning for him or her. For example, if the child enjoys swinging, a small piece of chain similar to what the child would hold onto while swinging may be used to symbolize the act of going to the playground to swing. It is important to use an actual object that the child interacts with, not a miniature or visual representation of the entire object. A calendar box provides a way to use these symbols to identify what is going to happen at a particular point in the day. A spoon may be chosen as the symbol representing "lunchtime" in a calendar box, and other familiar objects that are encountered during the day can represent activities in the daily schedule. Helping the child pair the symbol with the activity is a precursor to communication and supports language learning. Once the symbol for the activity is learned, this symbol can then be paired with more abstract tactile symbols. The form of language to use with the symbol needs to be determined. If the child is nonverbal but can hear, the teacher can pair a spoken word with the activity and symbol. If the child cannot hear, sign language can be used rather than a spoken word.

If the child is capable of understanding the pairing of words with tactile symbols, he or she may be capable of beginning to learn an even more abstract representation: braille letters or words. Braille letters can be combined with the word, the activity, and the tactile symbol on calendar boxes and other symbol systems. It doesn't hurt to have the braille letters on the symbol from the beginning, but it may not be what the child initially attends to when interacting with the symbol. Instead, the teacher may decide to first focus attention on the object/symbol to represent the word and activity, and add the braille word or letters later, as the child begins to be more exposed to braille in his or her environment. The child will then develop an understanding that braille has some meaning that represents the activities or objects (for example, the word *frog* in braille represents the actual animal in the classroom terrarium). The teacher can then begin to fade out the use of objects (that is, decrease dependence on objects as symbols for activities) and increase the exposure to braille as a way of introducing the concept of symbolic expressive language. When braille is put on the labels for objects and activities that are meaningful to the child, he or she learns that the object has a name, and that the braille word stands for the object or the activity.

Matthew's involvement in decorating his word box and putting the words in it is an important step for him. Because he now appears to have an understanding of what a word is, he may want the word *frog* to be the first word in his word box. Most likely, his teacher will suggest *Matthew* as the next word to put in, along with *Mr. Nobody,* of course. Remember that there are no hard and fast rules about which words to introduce when. Teachers should be attuned to the children for guidance in which words to introduce and when to introduce them. With these words, the teacher can begin to help Matthew play discrimination games like those suggested in Part 1. The teacher can also search through the list of Matthew's key words to see whether there are any other words that begin with *f* or *m* and start to introduce these to Matthew in a meaningful way. For example, one of Matthew's key words is *Mom,* which is what Matthew calls his mother. The teacher can talk to Matthew about *Mom* and be sure that he can relate to the word itself, and then introduce the word as one to include in the games. Since it begins with *m,* like *Matthew,* he will have to use something other than the first letter to distinguish the two words. *Mom* is a short word and *Matthew* is a long word, especially since Matthew's teacher has opted for uncontracted braille with Matthew at this point, so length could be the distinguishing factor.

Matthew has no physical impairments that would prevent his learning good tactile perception and letter recognition skills, so these can be built into his program just as they would with a learner like Brianna. The tracking exercises that are developed for him (such as those described in Part 1 of this book) merely need to reflect his interests. The teacher may want to begin helping him learn to track with a story about the frog escaping from his home. The word *frog* can be placed somewhere on a page of lines of dots 2-5, and Matthew would need to track the lines to find how far the frog has gotten from his home, which could be represented by four full cells on the left side of the page (see Figure 6). Letter recognition skills would begin with *f* and *m,* which are tactilely distinct and so would be suitable letters to begin with.

Assessing phonemic awareness will be more difficult with Matthew, since he currently has little expressive language. Matthew's teacher will

FIGURE 6: **Frog Escapes From Home**

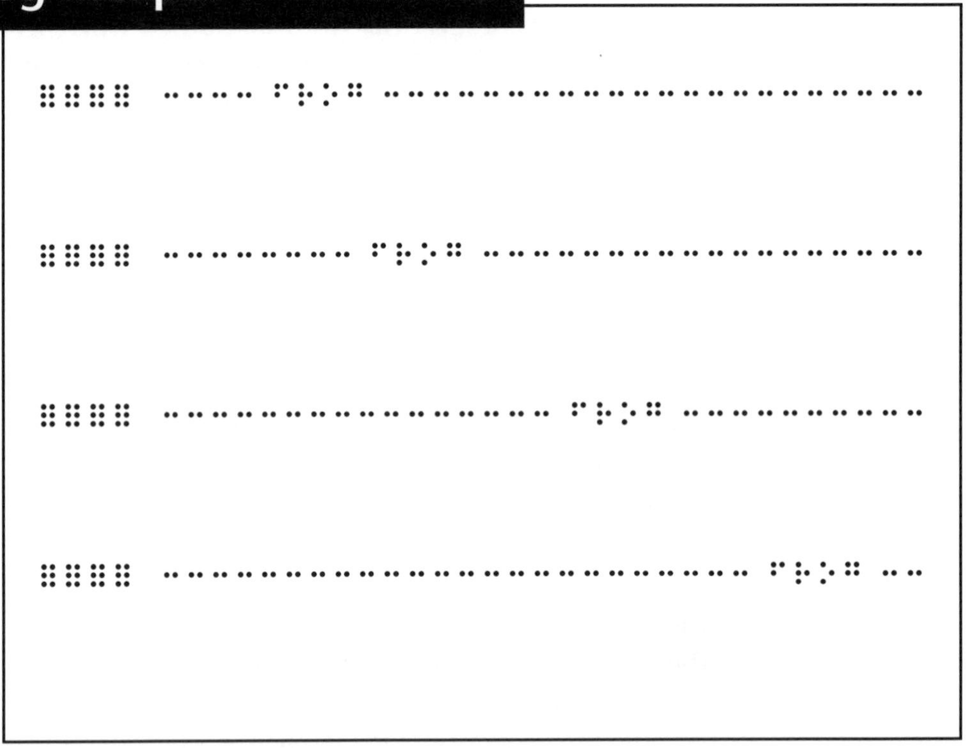

⠿⠿⠿⠿ ⠄⠄⠄⠄⠄⠄ ⠠⠋⠗⠕⠛ ⠄⠄⠄⠄⠄⠄⠄⠄⠄⠄⠄⠄⠄⠄⠄⠄⠄⠄⠄⠄⠄⠄⠄⠄⠄⠄⠄⠄⠄⠄⠄⠄⠄⠄⠄⠄

⠿⠿⠿⠿ ⠄⠄⠄⠄⠄⠄⠄⠄⠄⠄ ⠠⠋⠗⠕⠛ ⠄⠄⠄⠄⠄⠄⠄⠄⠄⠄⠄⠄⠄⠄⠄⠄⠄⠄⠄⠄⠄⠄⠄⠄⠄⠄⠄⠄

⠿⠿⠿⠿ ⠄⠄⠄⠄⠄⠄⠄⠄⠄⠄⠄⠄⠄⠄⠄⠄⠄⠄ ⠠⠋⠗⠕⠛ ⠄⠄⠄⠄⠄⠄⠄⠄⠄⠄⠄⠄

⠿⠿⠿⠿ ⠄⠄⠄⠄⠄⠄⠄⠄⠄⠄⠄⠄⠄⠄⠄⠄⠄⠄⠄⠄⠄⠄⠄⠄⠄⠄ ⠠⠋⠗⠕⠛ ⠄⠄⠄

want to consult with a speech therapist to assist in this aspect of his program. Using his key words as the beginning for sounds and patterns will help Matthew. Most likely, the assessment and instruction will occur simultaneously in a form of diagnostic teaching.

The remainder of the steps in the functional braille literacy approach can be followed with Matthew without deviating from the process described in Part 1. Record keeping will be extremely important with Matthew as with any of these at risk learners. As he learns new concepts, the words connected with them should become part of his key word vocabulary. As he begins to talk more, the words he speaks should be included in his word box, and the stories written should include his own expressions. Making reading and writing real for Matthew are the most important steps to helping him become literate.

Learners with Multiple Impairments, Including Physical Impairments

NELITA

Nelita is 18 and totally blind due to traumatic brain injury from a car accident at age 10. The same accident left her with slurred speech and the use of only her left hand.

Nelita's parents had moved several times since her accident and her schooling had been sporadic. Nelita's current teacher had been teaching Nelita for approximately a year, and had been using a traditional approach to teaching Nelita to read and write braille. Nelita was making very slow progress, however, and was very resistant to learning to read braille. She had learned most of the letters of the alphabet, but no contractions, and had little motivation to use her brailler or to read the stories that her teacher had located for her. Prior to her accident, Nelita had always enjoyed reading. Her parents had tried to urge her on by providing stories that had previously been her favorites, but Nelita was frustrated because she was unable to read the words.

On one day that was particularly frustrating, Nelita's teacher decided to try a functional approach with her. She asked Nelita what words she might really want to read. Nelita surprised the teacher by saying "blue!" in a loud, angry tone of voice. (Nelita's mother indicated afterward that this had been Nelita's favorite color before the accident.) Nelita's teacher brailled the word *blue* on a word card for her, and Nelita then said "cat." (Nelita's family had just acquired a kitten.) The teacher immediately brailled cat on a word card and gave it to Nelita. She then joked with Nelita that maybe the cat was a blue cat. Nelita smiled and put the two word cards next to each other and read "blue cat." She then quietly chuckled to herself. That afternoon she dictated to her teacher about ten more words that she wanted to read.

Nelita's attitude toward reading gradually changed. Using the talking card reader with the cards in her word box became a favorite activity, and she began to ask for time to write stories that her teacher would then transcribe into braille for her. Many of the stories were about her family and what she liked and didn't like. They were simple stories and involved a lot of repetition, which made it easy for her to read them on her own. She loved to write stories that didn't make sense, and would then read them and giggle over the silliness. She couldn't wait to take her storybook home to read the stories to her family. Her teacher initially kept the writing in uncontracted braille. Since Nelita had learned all the letters, this reinforced her letter recognition skills. As Nelita's reading and writing vocabulary increased, her teacher began to introduce contractions. Nelita was thrilled to learn that she could read a whole word with just one letter, as in the whole-word contractions (which use only the alphabet letters).

Nelita's teacher showed her how to use a braille notetaker in a one-handed mode, and Nelita began to write her own stories, which she would then listen to as well as read when they were printed out. Her teacher was able to use a variety of methods to improve her tracking and increase the number of braille contractions she was able to read and write.

Learners who have multiple impairments that include physical impairments need to be assessed as to whether they are physically capable of reading braille. In Nelita's case, her physical impairment slowed her down, because she could only use one hand to read and write braille, but it did not prevent her from reading tactilely.

On average, one-handed reading is slower than reading with both hands, so it is particularly important that the reader have accurate character recognition. Teaching good tactile perception and letter recognition skills is an important part of the approach. It is especially important to use a nonslip material under the braille with a one-handed reader, since the hand that is reading cannot also hold the paper.

Nelita's phonemic awareness and phonics skills were still intact. With some children who have multiple impairments, this may not be the case. The phonemic awareness assessment and activities may take a much greater amount of time than it does with students who do not have additional disabilities, but they will be reinforced by the reading activities. Concept development will also be a huge part of the curriculum leading toward emergent literacy for these learners. Without a strong foundation in basic concepts of how the world works, students will have difficulty understanding the meaning of what they read.

Adaptations are available for learners with physical impairments to help them with developing the skills of writing, as long as they have the use of one of their hands. For example, there are extended keys for the Perkins braillers, a special unimanual Perkins brailler, one-handed modes with various braille notetakers, electronic braillers that can be used with one hand (such as the Mountbatten) (see the Resources Section). There are also ways to make it easier for learners to put paper in their braillers without the use of both hands.

Nelita's teacher used a cardboard box that sat behind her Perkins brailler and was perfectly level with the area where the paper would be inserted. Nelita would lift up the paper release knobs on her brailler to open the spring that would receive the paper. She would then place her sheet of paper on the box and slide it into the Perkins as far as it would go, with one hand. Holding the paper in place with her index and middle fingers toward the right-hand side of the brailler, Nelita would then release the knobs with her thumb so that the paper was secure. Then she could roll the paper into the brailler and lock it in place using the left-hand knob on the machine. Nelita had more difficulty with the mechanics of writing because it was a slower process with the use of only one hand. But, she loved the creative aspect of writing stories and this is what motivated her to continue to learn more and more braille. She enjoyed reading the stories she and her teacher created, and read them over and over. The repeated readings helped her recognition and her fluency.

Shortly after beginning to use the functional approach with Nelita, her teacher realized that Nelita had the capability and now the desire to be literate in braille. She was no longer as frustrated as she had been and was eager to read and write braille. Although the teacher had not previously had success using a traditional approach with Nelita, she determined that when Nelita had learned all of her contractions she would try to move her into a modified academic approach. She began keeping track of the contractions to which Nelita was exposed and that she was reading. She began looking for materials that utilized high-interest low-vocabulary readers and for some books on cats, since she knew that Nelita was very fond of her pet.

Learners with Deaf-Blindness

JENNA

Jenna is 8 years old and has a severe hearing loss in both ears. She has light perception only, although on some days her vision seems to be better, allowing her to recognize high-contrast shapes and simple illustrations such as those her teacher uses on her calendar. The cause of her deaf-blindness is noted in her records as prematurity.

In preschool, Jenna was always disruptive. She had favorite activities, such as playing in the ball pit (a box of colored balls in which a small child can bury herself, often found at indoor-play centers), and she would throw temper tantrums when she was not allowed to do them. When Jenna reached school age, her teacher instituted a calendar system with her, helped her develop some tactile signs (such as her name sign), and began to use the things that Jenna liked to do as a reward for good behavior during the other activities. She also expanded Jenna's repertoire of favorite activities to include riding a tricycle and even began taking her bowling with an older group of students. Jenna liked to get as close to the pins as possible and would shriek with laughter and jump up and down when the pins went down with a crash! She also liked to help set the pins back up although she was not able to set them up correctly and required considerable guidance.

Recently Jenna was tested for use of an auditory trainer with an FM system, and this was implemented in her classroom, a classroom exclusively for deaf-blind children at a specialized school for children who are blind. FM amplification systems transmit the teacher's voice directly to the student at a constant level, insuring that the teacher's voice is heard above the level of background noise, regardless of the teacher's distance from the student. FM systems consist of a microphone and a transmitter (or a combination), a receiver, and some method of routing sounds from the receiver to the student's ear. The teacher wears the microphone and transmitter. The transmitter changes the electrical signal from the microphone into an FM signal, which is sent to the student's receiver. Wherever the teacher stands in the classroom, the student hears the teacher's voice as if it were coming from just a few inches away. Jenna responded very well to the auditory trainer and learned to distinguish her name and simple commands and greetings. Her behavior is now under control and Jenna is demonstrating that she is capable of learning to communicate using tactile signs and objects. Her teacher decided to introduce Jenna to braille reading and writing but did not know where to start because of Jenna's dual impairments.

The teacher began by labeling everything in Jenna's environment with braille. She put Jenna's name on everything that was hers—her desk, her calendar, and her cane to begin with. Because she was using objects paired with a raised-line, high-contrast, black-and-white picture for the various activities Jenna liked to do, she also placed braille labels on these as well. Initially, Jenna would find the braille and immediately pick off the labels. She appeared to dislike the feel of the labels or the dots, especially on her belongings. She tolerated them better when they were in more general areas of the classroom.

The teacher also began collecting the vocabulary words that she knew Jenna understood. She realized that the hardest task would be to help Jenna pair the symbols and word signs with the braille in order to begin some form of written communication. The teacher brailled word cards for Jenna and had Jenna take them with her to various locations. She matched the word cards with the braille labels on the signs so that Jenna could begin to see the connection. For instance, when Jenna was going to the school nurse to get her morning medications, her teacher would give her the word card for nurse, help Jenna make the sign for nurse and have Jenna pick up the pill container that was Jenna's tactile symbol for going to the nurse. When they got to the nurse's office, her teacher would show Jenna that the word on the word card and the sign for nurse were the same. (Jenna understood the concepts of "same" and "different" and their corresponding signs in sign language.)

The teacher also wanted to teach Jenna that names could be written. She began with Jenna's name, the names of the other students, and the names of the teachers with whom Jenna interacted. Jenna knew her own name sign, a *J* formed near her cheek. Jenna had also easily learned the signs for the different teachers, and was learning the name signs of the other student with whom she sometimes interacted (she still preferred to play by herself rather than with others). The teacher concentrated on teaching Jenna that the braille word was her name. She kept placing and replacing the labels on Jenna's belongings after Jenna picked them off, showing Jenna the word card with her name on it, and making the sign for Jenna. One day, Jenna brought her teacher the word card with her name on it, and pointed to herself and made her name sign. Her teacher immediately took Jenna's hand and shook it up and down for "yes." Then she gave Jenna a big hug! She then went to Jenna's cane and had Jenna feel the braille label on it. Jenna again signed her name. The teacher felt that this was a real breakthrough and hoped that Jenna would be able to make more progress in learning to read words that were important to her from that point on.

Literacy cannot occur without language:

> The challenge of learning to communicate is perhaps the greatest one that children who are deaf-blind face. It is also the greatest opportunity, since communication and language hold the power to make their thoughts, needs, and desires known. The ability to use words can also open up worlds beyond the reach of their fingertips. . . . [Miles, 2000]

Deaf-blindness imposes dual constraints on learning language. Students who are visually impaired but who can hear are familiar with the sounds of words and language. They may have difficulty understanding concepts because of their visual impairment, but they are able to communicate using spoken language. Visually impaired students who are nonverbal for various reasons but who can hear and understand receptive language have a distinct advantage in the acquisition of literacy over those who cannot hear. The teacher has only to determine what words are within the child's experience to know where to begin.

With a child who is deaf-blind, the teacher actually has to *create* the key vocabulary. As Qualls-Mitchell (2002) points out, "Part of the progression of learning to read for students is building a significant glossary

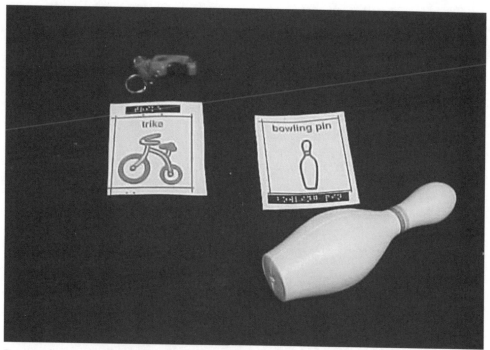

Examples from Jenna's calendar system. Actual objects, such as a keychain with a small tricycle that Jenna associates with bike riding and a bowling pin, are paired with high-contrast pictures that have the words on them in print and braille, to represent Jenna's favorite activities.

of words, bringing meaning to reading using previous knowledge . . ." (p. 77). Indeed, with children who are deaf-blind, the process of teaching them to read itself builds their vocabulary and gives them language. For example, with Jenna, providing her with the written words for her tricycle and the bowling pin helps her understand that objects have names and that they can be represented in sign language as well as in braille. The teacher must become familiar with the child's environment and what the child experiences. Knowing what is familiar to the child allows the teacher to create a literacy program that is meaningful to the student. Working with the family is particularly important when the child cannot communicate what is going on at home.

Creating meaningful tracking and tactile perception exercises for a student such as Jenna will be challenging. The fact that Jenna can now recognize her name suggests that her teacher can begin trying these activities with her. For example, the teacher might pretend for the first tracking

FIGURE 7: Jenna in the Ball Pit

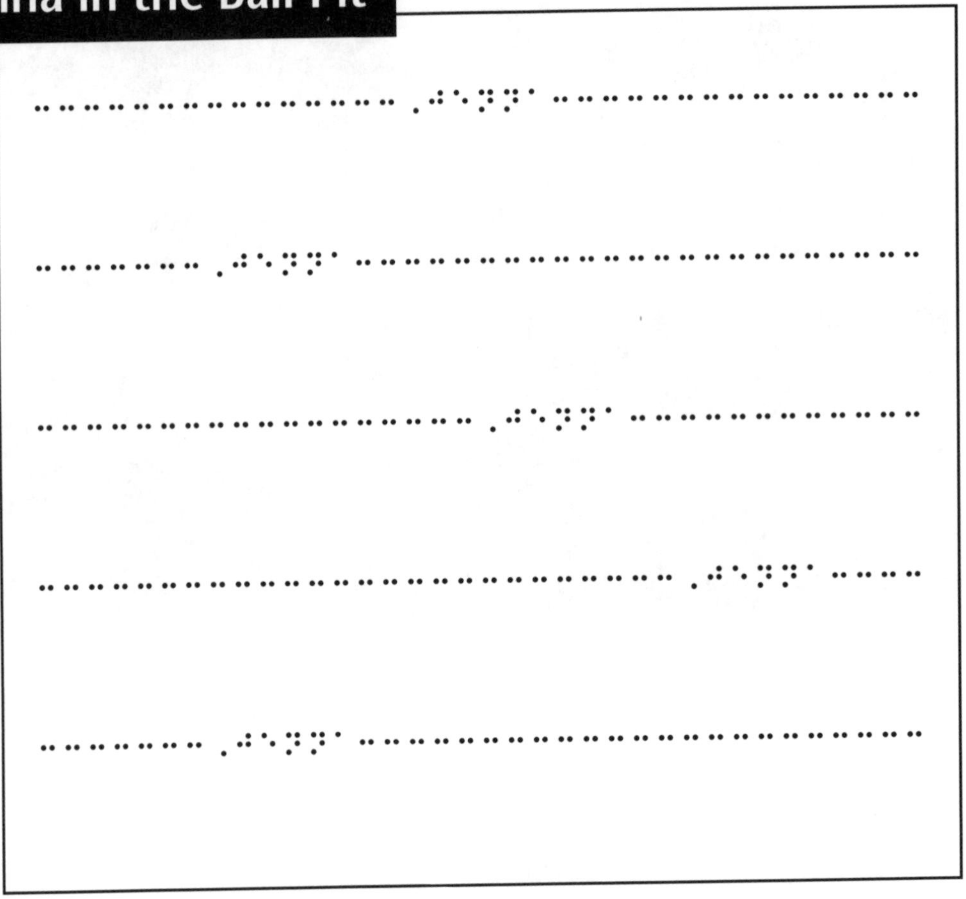

exercise that Jenna is in the ball pit and that she must be found (see Figure 7). This requires that Jenna understands how to pretend that the ball pit is the line of braille and also understands the concept of "find." Before the tracking exercise is undertaken, the teacher will need to be sure that Jenna has the language for the task. Jenna's teacher can introduce each of the other steps simultaneously, with constant assessment of Jenna's progress. The most important part of designing a program for Jenna is to be sure to relate all the activities to the key word vocabulary and to also use the activities to expand her vocabulary.

Making books and stories with the child based directly on the child's routines and experiences will be especially important for emergent literacy. These books can be "illustrated" with actual objects labeled with the braille words. For example, after Jenna's eighth birthday party, her mother and teacher created a book with Jenna that told in simple, repetitive language the story of her birthday party. As "illustrations," they included an uninflated balloon, a small paper plate, a small toy that the children had been given, a party hat (slightly flattened), and other real objects from the party. Jenna enjoyed "reading" this story over and over, and would sit with her mother or her teacher and go page by page, first feeling the page, then having the word signed to her, and then tracking over the braille word again and examining the objects and their accompanying braille labels. Sometimes she would make the sign for the object before reading the word again, and sometimes she would read and sign several times in succession before moving on to the next page. Each time, her teacher or her mother would let her know that she was "reading" correctly and praise her. It was obvious to everyone that Jenna was catching on to language and reading.

School-Aged Learners Who Are Adventitiously Blinded

LEANDRAE

Leandrae is 17 years old and has retinitis pigmentosa. She had been able to read print through her sophomore year in high school, at which time she experienced a sudden dramatic loss of vision. Leandrae had never been exposed to braille and when she started to learn it, she was very afraid that she would not be able to read it. She had been a good reader until her vision loss, and she was concerned that she would never be able to get to the same point with braille. She was discouraged that her fingers just did not seem to be able to recognize the difference in the various braille letters. Her teacher decided to use a functional approach to convince her that she would be able to succeed.

Leandrae's teacher asked her what words she would most like to learn to read. Leandrae chose her own name, and then her best friend's name, Cleo. The teacher brailled word cards for both names and printed the names on the backs of the cards. She showed Leandrae how to position the cards on the nonslip mat, and made sure that Leandrae understood how important it was to keep her fingers moving from left to right over the letters.

Leandrae took the word cards home and came back the next day saying she could tell them apart and she also knew the contraction for *and* which was in her name. She came in with several other names she wanted to try to learn to read. Her teacher suggested that she help her write the names herself on the Perkins brailler, and showed her how to make the lead-in lines that would help her develop smooth tracking skills for the words on the cards. She showed her how to use other clues to identify words, such as the length of the word and the dominant letters (those that are easy to feel and that stand out in a word).

Leandrae came back the following day having learned all the other names she had selected, but with a different concern. This wasn't really reading. She was afraid she would never be able to learn everything to keep up with her classmates. And, she wanted to be able to recognize numbers so that she could retrieve her friends' telephone numbers. Her teacher first started with the numbers. She gave Leandrae flash cards of the numbers 0–9. Each flash card had the number sign and one of the numerals 0–9 brailled on one side, and the corresponding printed number on the other side, so Leandrae's mother could help her learn the numbers. She also gave her some tracking activities with lines of each number in order. Then she created some tracking pages on which there were lead-in and lead-out lines of dots 2-5 with just one number for each line. She presented the numbers in order first, and then out of order as a test (see Figure 8). As she told Leandrae, she didn't want to make it seem like she wasn't really reading!

Leandrae came in the next day having memorized all the single-digit numbers. At this point, her teacher asked her for the area codes and telephone numbers of several of her friends. She isolated the area codes and created some tracking sheets so that Leandrae could work on identifying only these. Then she added the next three digits to the area codes, and then the four following digits. She then created flash cards for the numbers Leandrae had identified. She had Leandrae

FIGURE 8: **Leandrae's Number Tracking Exercise**

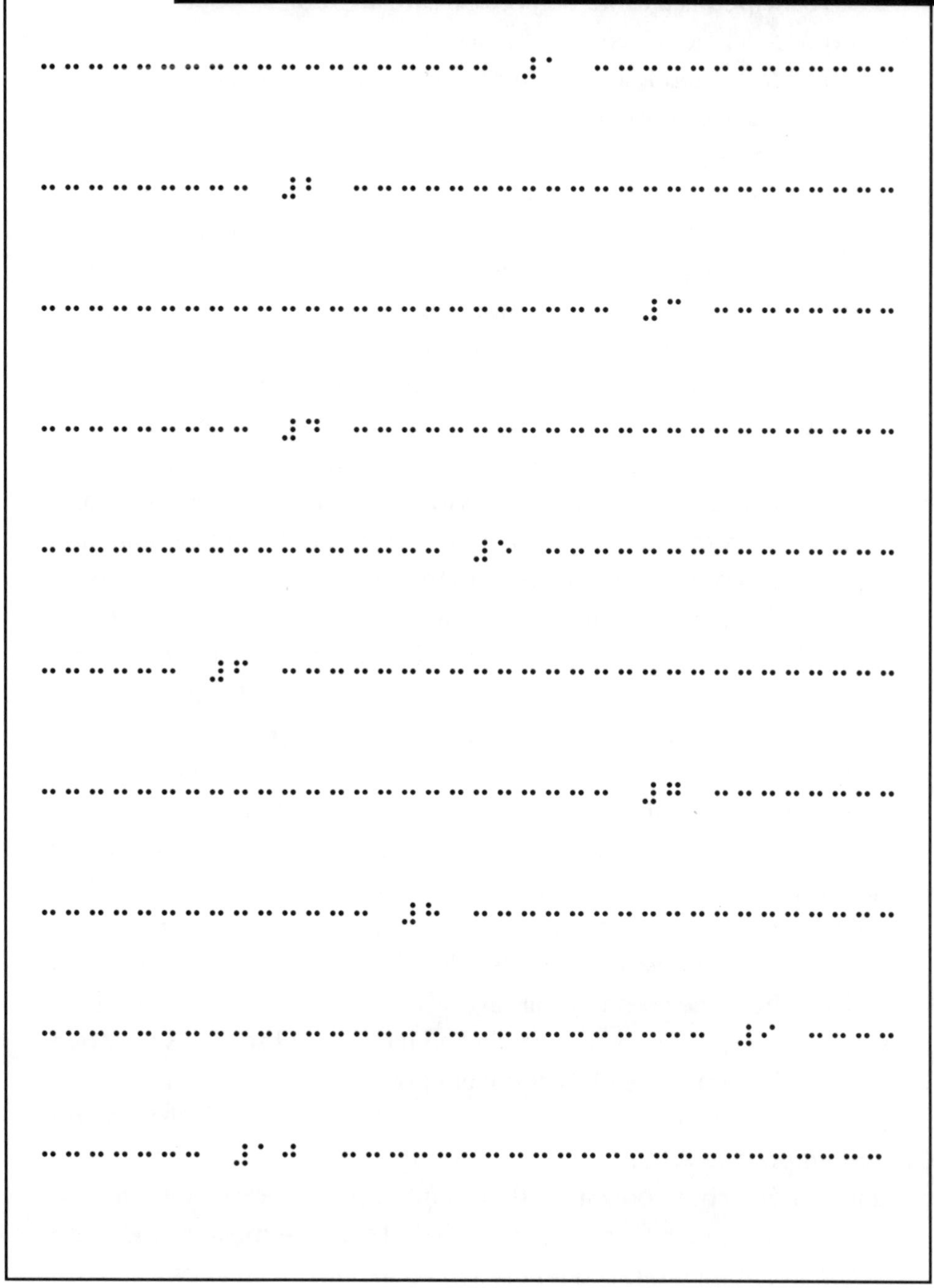

select the names of her friends from her word box, and asked her to match each name with the correct telephone number. Then her teacher helped Leandrae begin to create an address book for herself using 3" × 5" index cards and a file box.

To address Leandrae's concerns that she was not really reading, her teacher decided to isolate several of the letters in her friends' names to help her begin to recognize them. She started with some tracking exercises for each of the letters, incorporating them into lines on the pages. The letters she chose initially were *l, a, r, c, o,* as well as *d* from *Donna,* and *b, i,* and *n* from *Brian.* Leandrae quickly caught on to recognizing each of these letters, especially since she had already learned the numerals 1–10 which also represent the letters a–j.

Leandrae mentioned that now when she read her friend's names, she felt like she was really reading. Her teacher then suggested that Leandrae use the letters she had learned to create words to practice at home. Leandrae created word cards for *car, card, no, ill, darn, loan,* and *barn.* Because four of the words Leandrae created contained an "ar" sign, her teacher showed her how to form that contraction when writing, and then created some tracking activities for Leandrae to use with the "ar" sign to help her read it. She also taught Leandrae the initial-letter whole-word contractions for *like, rather, can, do, but,* and *not,* formed with just the letters *l, r, c, d, b,* and *n* which she now knew.

Leandrae now had a number of words to practice reading. The teacher recorded which letters, contractions, and whole words Leandrae had now been exposed to, and prepared a small quiz, which she gave Leandrae the next day. She also brought out her copy of the *Mangold Developmental Program of Tactile Perception and Braille Letter Recognition* to use with Leandrae. She also began to use some initial activities from the commercially available curriculum *Braille Too,* which was devised specifically for middle and high school students who had formerly been print readers and were now starting braille instruction.

Leandrae's teacher could see that Leandrae was already developing a more positive attitude toward learning braille from using the functional approach, in only a short amount of time, and she intended to be ready with materials that would help Leandrae move quickly into becoming as fluent a reader in braille as she had been in print.

Learners who have previously used print for reading and writing often find it frustrating when they start to learn braille. Although they may previously have been fluent readers, they are now appalled to find that they feel and sound like first graders when they read. They may feel that they will never learn to read again, and may be discouraged from even trying, in case they fail. Teachers who push these learners to use only an auditory mode of reading, without encouraging them to learn braille, often only reinforce the leaners' fears that they will not be successful with braille. Learners who are adjusting to vision loss may not have the motivation to try to learn something new and may be discouraged because it seems so difficult. Teachers need to help them learn to read again for their self-esteem as well as for their future education.

The functional approach is often less threatening to these learners. It shows them that braille is a tool that they can use even while they are still learning it and are not yet fluent. Leandrae's concern was that she didn't feel as though she were really reading, and she wanted to move more quickly. The approach did what it needed to; it convinced her that she would be able to read braille and made her want to keep working on her braille reading.

A teacher may decide not to create a braille-rich environment for a learner like Leandrae. These learners are aware of where they would find print in the environment and know what words mean. But the step of creating word boxes and key words should not be skipped. It forces the learner to consider what is important to him or her, and using key words with personal meaning for the student makes braille reading more meaningful. Since the words are familiar and are chosen by the learner, the motivation to learn to read them is already there.

Perhaps the most important step for this group of learners is teaching them good tactile perception and letter recognition skills. Learners who are allowed to scrub will not increase their reading speed. They need help to develop good tracking and letter recognition skills with materials that have been designed to decrease the need to scrub. Learners need to be provided with an explanation of the ways that accomplished braille readers move their hands when reading. They need to be taught that smooth left-to-right movement with both hands eventually provides for more speed. They may need to be told to consciously keep both hands moving over a word even if they do not recognize it at first and then go back over it again and again, until they can discern the features of the letters and words. Teachers can help by directing learners to the parts of the characters that are critical features.

Since many if not most learners who are adventitiously blinded have already learned to read print, it is not necessary to provide instruction in phonemic awareness and phonics, unless something in the initial assessment indicates that the learner had previously had a problem in this area. It is important, however, to provide this particular group with information about how braille reading and print reading differ.

Leandre's teacher explained to her that unlike print reading, braille is approached in a more sequential manner. Therefore, Leandrae needed to be accurate in her recognition of each new character learned before moving on to the next character; to increase her rate of accuracy, she needed to practice. In addition, it was important that she control her urge to move her fingers up and down on the characters, even though it seemed that this would enable her to feel them better. Leandrae's teacher explained that this "scrubbing" eventually results in slower reading and that Leandrae should practice keeping her fingers moving from left to right over the characters until she was able to recognize the letters.

Another thing that Leandrae discovered early on was that her fingers were frequently becoming desensitized. She would initially have total accuracy when identifying numbers or letters, and then suddenly feel as if she could not identify anything. Leandrae realized that this meant she needed to take a break.

Leandrae's teacher provided her with much of this information to enable her to check herself and her progress. She taught Leandrae how to create her own tracking sheets for letters and words that she wanted to learn and how to pace herself and stop when she needed to take breaks. Leandrae enjoyed having the opportunity to work at her own pace. Having control over her learning also helped Leandrae feel proud of what she had accomplished.

Learners like Leandrae often need blocks of time devoted only to reading, and these blocks of time may need to be found on school holidays or during the summer. Building fluency in braille reading can be difficult for these learners because fluency doesn't come automatically as a result of having previous reading experience or the ability to recognize individual braille letters. Often, familiar children's stories are useful for building fluency, because the learners can use their prior knowledge to anticipate and predict what the words are. Repeated readings of stories also help to build fluency. Learners like Leandrae need extensive time spent reading to develop the fluency they need to be fast enough to keep up with their peers. Teachers of visually impaired students may need to advocate during the student's IEP meeting for this time for a learner and work with the learner to find the best ways to find blocks of time that can be devoted to reading and writing practice.

Because the functional approach does not introduce letters or contractions in any precise order, record keeping is extremely important. Accurate records allow the teacher to know what contractions and letters a learner has mastered. Once a student like Leandrae is convinced that she can learn to read using braille, a traditional approach like the program *Braille Too* (Hepker & Coquillette, 1995) might then be implemented. This program is designed with older students in mind and will ensure that they learn all the contractions in the code.

Adult Learners Who Are Adventitiously Blinded

MRS. BEADLE

Mrs. Beadle recently had significant vision loss resulting from macular degeneration. Even before this loss, however, she was concerned because the macular degeneration prevented her from reading the numbers in the elevator in her apartment building. She had gotten off on the wrong floor several times. She knew that there were braille numbers in the elevator and on the number panels out-

Mrs. Beadle reads the floor numbers in her apartment elevator.

side the elevator. When a rehabilitation teacher came to work with her, Mrs. Beadle asked her whether she could help her learn to read the numbers in braille so that she wouldn't worry about getting off on the wrong floor again.

Mrs. Beadle's rehabilitation teacher developed some tracking exercises (see Figure 9) and flash cards for numbers. Within a short time, Mrs. Beadle had learned the number sign and numbers 1 through 5 as well as *L* for lobby and *g* for ground floor, where the laundry room was. The rehabilitation teacher pointed out that without intending to, she had also learned the letters in her last name, since the numbers 1–5 also represent the letters *a–e*.

Mrs. Beadle had not thought that she would use braille for anything other than the elevator, but her success with numbers coupled with her rehabilitation teacher's encouragement convinced her that she might be able to use it for labeling some items around her home. The reha-

FIGURE 9: Mrs. Beadle's Number Tracking Exercise

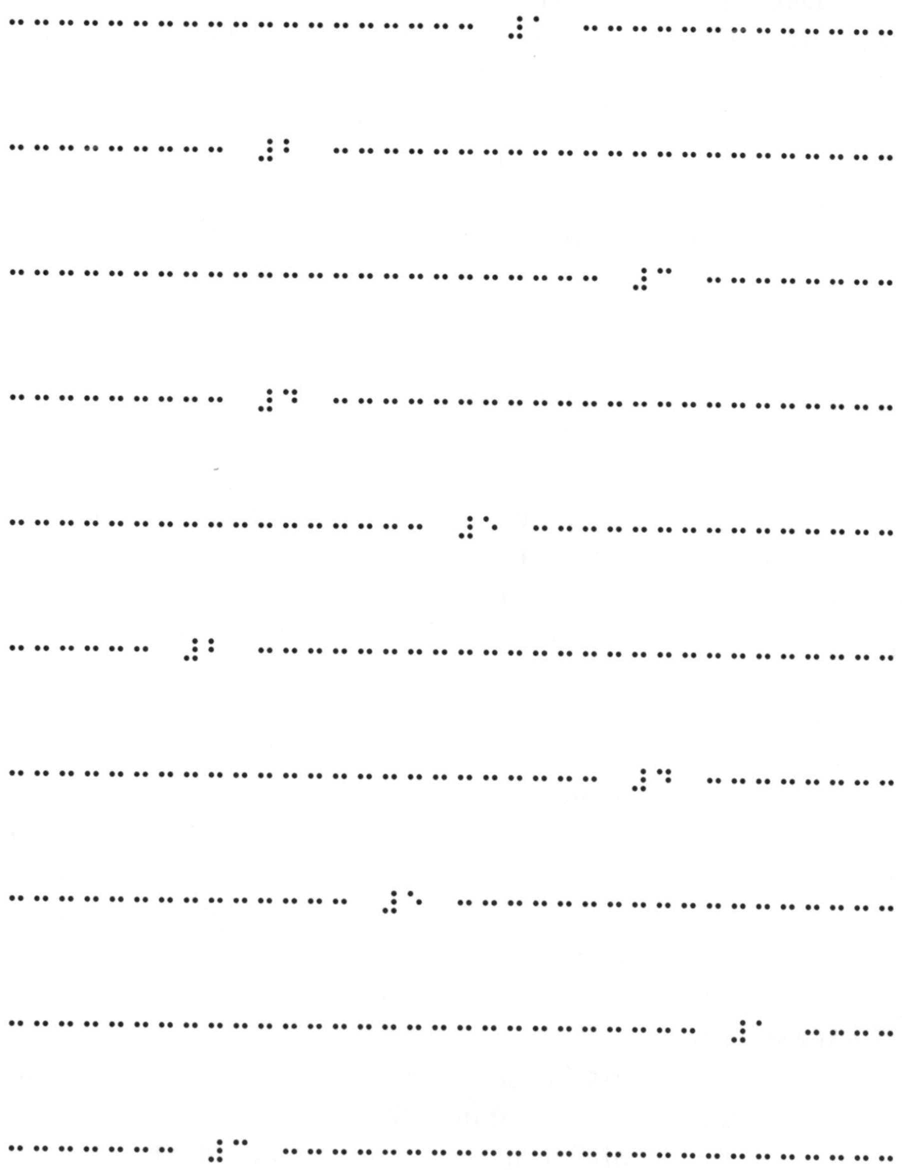

bilitation teacher began working with Mrs. Beadle to use the letters and numbers to develop a labeling system for Mrs. Beadle's clothes. Mrs. Beadle used only a few letters and numbers on her microwave to help her identify the touch panels that she used most often. At that point, Mrs. Beadle was recognizing the numbers and letters easily and accurately and her rehabilitation teacher suggested that she might consider trying to learn more of the braille numbers and letters so that she could write telephone numbers and names in braille for her address book. Mrs. Beadle was pleased that she could use braille to this extent.

Once she had the accuracy she needed, Mrs. Beadle and her rehabilitation teacher began to work on labeling her medicines using numbers and a labeling code that Mrs. Beadle and her rehabilitation teacher devised.

Using a functional approach to braille literacy makes ultimate sense with adults. Adults want to see results immediately. They want to see that something they spend time learning can be put to good use. If after a few lessons they are able to use braille in their daily lives, even if they are not actually reading and writing, they will have more faith in their abilities to progress beyond this limited use of braille and are then more likely to attempt to learn to read. Most of these adults will already have learned to read print. Many older adults do not relish having to undergo what they may consider to be an arduous task in order to be able to read again. Unfortunately, many older adults have the impression that braille is something difficult to learn and something they would not want to invest a lot of time in. So, bringing braille into their daily lives in a functional way is a great motivator for them to learn more.

The key with the functional approach for adults is to keep asking them what they want to do next. Mrs. Beadle has learned to read elevator numbers, has labeled her clothing and her microwave, and can now label her medicines. She feels confident in her tactile recognition of the numbers and her tactile code. This is the time for her rehabilitation teacher to ask about other things Mrs. Beadle would like to do in the area of reading or writing. Having had success in one area of literacy will help her feel less tentative about moving into another area.

A rehabilitation teacher should get a good idea of the learner's previous literacy level to determine whether reading skills are already in place. The initial teaching tasks should really be directed by the adult. Instead of creating stories, the adult who is visually impaired may want to be sure that he or she can create a grocery list and read it back to someone over the telephone or read it while shopping with a friend. These tasks may not even involve braille. However, the rehabilitation teacher can bring in the element of using braille when appropriate and help the adult to understand its potential.

When working with adults, as with other learners, it is important to include all the steps of the approach and not to skip proper tracking and letter identification skills. The rehabilitation teacher can use what he or she knows about the learner to create tracking activities that will be meaningful and not insulting to the learner. Adequate explanation of the importance of smooth tracking can be explained for this learner in the same way that it was with Leandrae.

Although with a younger learner like Leandrae a teacher may move her into a more traditional approach as early as possible, rehabilitation teachers may want to be sensitive to the pace the adult learner is comfortable with. How much braille reading a learner may want to explore will depend on success with the program attempted. It may also depend on how much reading the learner did before losing vision. When it comes time to make the transition into a more traditional reading approach, the rehabilitation teacher can choose from a number of commercially available curricula devised for teaching braille to adults who have acquired a visual impairment, such as those from the American Printing House for the Blind (see the Resources section).

Learners for Whom English Is a Second Language

TRAN NGUYEN

Tran Nguyen came with his family to the United States from Vietnam after living in a refugee camp in Thailand. Tran was 6 years old when his family fled Vietnam. During their escape through Cambodia, he had been hit in his right eye with flying debris from a landmine explosion. He lost his vision in the other eye shortly thereafter as the result of an infection. Tran was 11 years old when his family came to the United States and had not received any formal education. Tran and his family spoke very little English. The school district placed him in a special education resource room where the emphasis would be on independent living skills, because his test results indicated that he was developmentally delayed. His special education resource room teacher felt that he did not have a cognitive impairment and should be doing more academic work, but did not know where to start with him, because he had no ability to read or write and was not speaking any English either at home or in the classroom.

Tran's teacher of visually impaired students first consulted with a teacher of English as a second language (ESL) in the school district and brought the ESL teacher onto Tran's individualized education program (IEP) team. From the ESL teacher, she received information about what sounds Tran might have difficulty with and exercises she could use to help him recognize and pronounce these sounds. She was able to locate an interpreter within the community who helped her interview Tran's family regarding his favorite foods, games, and activities. This information was later incorporated into the stories she and Tran wrote together for him to read.

Tran's independent living skills curriculum was also the basis for a large portion of his vocabulary words. Tran was very quiet initially, but one day he approached his teacher and spoke an entire English sentence. The ESL teacher explained that he had now passed through what is called the "preproduction" or "silent" period of second-language development. With the approval of the ESL teacher, Tran's teacher of visually impaired students began by using Tran's home and school environment to teach him the English names of things that were familiar to him. She began his braille instruction at the same time, by pairing the braille with the English words. These became the basis of his word box. He learned *brush your teeth, get dressed, shirt, button,* and *shoes,* along with many other words and expressions that he then learned to read in braille. The teacher paired the nouns and verbs to make short sentences or phrases, such as *touch your nose* or *bend your elbow.* She helped Tran learn how to use the Perkins brailler and the slate and stylus to write out his daily schedule and to begin to write stories about himself and his daily activities.

Tran's teacher of visually impaired students began using the *Mangold Developmental Program of Tactile Perception and Braille Letter Recognition* with him, and discovered that he could name the letters and identify each letter's sound in the initial position with very little difficulty. She discovered that he had been listening to *Sesame Street* on television and knew the names and sounds of the letters, but did not have any referent or symbol system to which to apply them. Tran and his teacher then began analyzing the words in his word box for the letters they contained. At this point, Tran's IEP team felt that he was ready to begin a more formal reading and writing program. However, his teachers continued to use a language experience approach with Tran to make his progression from Vietnamese to English and to braille reading and writing smoother. They also worked with Tran to identify unfamiliar concepts in stories to assist him in building vocabulary.

The steps in the functional approach could be followed fairly closely with Tran, once the hurdle of learning English was overcome. As with children who are deaf-blind, those who learn English as a second language have to make progress in learning the language before they can begin to apply that to learning to reading and writing, especially if they were not literate in their native language. Because initially they do not have the words, the functional approach often opens the door to literacy for them in a meaningful way. It allows them to bring their experiences to the task of learning to read and write in another language in the medium of braille.

Summary

The functional approach to learning to read and write using braille can be used successfully with a variety of learners. As demonstrated in this section, the approach is applied in a slightly different fashion with different types of learners. Teachers need to become familiar with the steps listed in Part 1 of this book to be sure that they are including all of them when working with an individual learner, either through direct instruction or assessment indicating that the learner already has the skills addressed in that step.

Teachers may feel that they should begin by using a traditional approach with learners and then switch to a functional approach if the traditional approach is not working. With groups of learners who tend to have particular trouble learning braille, such as those discussed in this chapter, however, it is most important that the instruction is meaningful to them. It is not necessary to begin instruction in a traditional approach before using a functional approach. In fact, implementing the functional approach from the very beginning is likely to ensure that the learner is interested and motivated. Moreover, a functional approach can flow readily into a more traditional approach. Teachers need to determine whether their students fit into any of the categories of at-risk learners described in this section, and should feel free to begin using a functional approach with them as soon as possible.

References

Adler, C. R. (Ed.). (2001). Put reading first: The research building blocks for teaching children to read. Kindergarten through grade 3. Jessup, MD: The Partnership for Reading. [Online] Available: <www.nifl.gov>.

Anderson, R. D., Hiebert, E. H., Scott, J. A., & Wilkinson, I. A. G. (1985). *Becoming a nation of readers. The report of the Commission on Reading.* Washington, DC: National Academy of Education, National Institute of Education.

Caton, H., Gordon, B., Pester, E., Roderick, C., & Modaressi, B. (1997). *The braille connection: A braille reading and writing program for former print users.* Louisville, KY: American Printing House for the Blind.

Caton, H., Pester, E., & Bradley, E. J. (1980). *Patterns: The primary braille reading program.* Louisville, KY: American Printing House for the Blind.

D'Andrea, F. M. (1997). Teaching braille to students with special needs. In D. P. Wormsley, & F. M. D'Andrea (Eds.), *Instructional Strategies for Braille Literacy* (pp. 145–188). New York: AFB Press.

Duffy, G. G., & Hoffman, J. V. (1999). In pursuit of an illusion: The flawed search for a perfect method. *The Reading Teacher, 53,* 10–16.

Hatlen, P. (2000). Historical perspectives. In M. C. Holbrook & A. J. Koenig (Eds.), *Foundations of education* (2nd Ed.): *Vol. I. History and theory of teaching children and youths with visual impairments* (pp. 1–54). New York: AFB Press.

Hepker, N., & Coquillette, S. C. (1995). *Braille too.* Cedar Rapids, IA: Grant Wood Area Education Agency.

Kame'enui, E. J., Simmons, D. C., Baker, S., Chard, D. J., Dickson, S. V., Gunn, B., Smith, S. B., Sprick, M., & Lin, S. J. (1997). Effective reading strategies for teaching beginning reading. In E. J. Kame'enui, & D. W. Carnine (Eds.), *Effective teaching strategies that accommodate diverse learners.* Columbus, OH: Merrill.

Kliewer, C., & Landis, D. (1999). Individualizing literacy instruction for young children with moderate to severe disabilities. *Exceptional Children, 66*(1), 85–100.

Koenig, A. J. & Holbrook, M. C. (1995). *Learning media assessment of students with visual impairments: A resource guide for teachers* (2nd ed.). Austin: Texas School for the Blind and Visually Impaired.

Kusajima, T. (1974). *Visual reading and braille reading: An experimental investigation of the physiology and psychology of visual and tactual reading.* New York: American Foundation for the Blind.

Lamb, G. (1996). Beginning braille: A whole-language based strategy. *Journal of Visual Impairment & Blindness, 92,* 184–189.

Leu, D. J., & Kinzer, C. K. (1991). *Effective reading instruction K–8* (2nd ed.). New York: Merrill.

Lowenfeld, B. (1973). *The visually handicapped child in school.* New York: John Day.

Mangold, S. S. (1989). *The Mangold developmental program of tactile perception and braille letter recognition.* Castro Valley, CA: Exceptional Teaching Aids.

Mason, J. M., & Au, K. H. (1990). *Reading instruction for today.* Glenview, IL: Scott Foresman.

Miles, B. (2000, July). *Overview on deafblindness. Connections beyond sight and sound: Maryland's project on deafblindness.* [Online] Available: <http://www.education.umd.edu/Depts/EDSP/Connections/db_definition.html>.

Millar, S. (1997). *Reading by touch.* London: Routledge.

Miller, W. H. (1995). *Alternative assessment techniques for reading and writing.* West Nyack, NY: The Center for Applied Research in Education.

Miller, W. H. (2001). *The reading teacher's survival kit.* West Nyack, NY: The Center for Applied Research in Education.

Moustafa, M. (1995). Children's productive phonological recoding. *Reading Research Quarterly, 30,* 464–476.

National Reading Panel (2000). *Teaching children to read: An evidence-based assessment of the scientific research literacy on reading and its implications for reading instruction.* [Online] Available: <http://www.nichd.nih.gov/publications/nrp/report.htm>.

Pester, E., Petrosko, J. M., & Poppe, K. J. (1994). Optimum size and spacing for introducing blind adults to the braille code. *RE:view, 26*(1), 15–22.

Purcell-Gates, V., Degener, S. C., Jacobson, E., & Soler, M. (2002). Impact of authentic adult literacy instruction on adult literacy practices. *Reading Research Quarterly, 37*(1), 70–92.

Qualls-Mitchell, P. (2002). Reading enhancement for deaf and hard-of-hearing children through multicultural empowerment. *The Reading Teacher, 56*(1), 76–84.

Rayner, K., Foorman, B. R., Perfetti, C. A., Pesetsky, D., & Seidenberg, M. S. (2002). How should reading be taught? *Scientific American,* March 2002, 84–91.

Rex, E. J., Koenig, A. J., Wormsley, D. P., & Baker, R. L. (1994). *Foundations of braille literacy.* New York: AFB Press.

Rodenburg, L. W. (1977). *Key to grade three braille.* Louisville, KY: American Printing House for the Blind.

Routman, R. (2003). *Reading essentials: The specifics you need to teach reading well.* Portsmouth, NH: Heinemann.

Sanford, L., & Burnett, R. (1997). *Functional vision and media assessment checklist.* Heritage, TN: Consultants for the Visually Impaired.

Simons, B. (1997). How to make a braille wave. In D. P. Wormsley & F. M. D'Andrea (Eds.), *Instructional Strategies for Braille Literacy* (pp. 324–326). New York: AFB Press.

Swenson, A. (1999). *Beginning with braille.* New York: AFB Press.

Texas primary reading inventory. (2003). Austin: [Online] Available: <http://www.txreadinginstruments.com>.

Vellutin, F. R., & Scanlon, D. M. (1987). Phonological coding, phonological awareness, and reading ability: Evidence from a longitudinal and experimental study. *Merrill-Palmer Quarterly, 33,* 321–363.

Warner, S. A. (1963). *Teacher.* New York: Simon & Schuster.

Wormsley, D. P. (1979). *The effects of a hand movement training program on the hand move-*

ments and reading rates of young braille read-ers. Ann Arbor, MI: University Microfilms International.

Wormsley, D. P. (2000). *Braille literacy curriculum.* Philadelphia, PA: Towers Press of Overbrook School for the Blind.

Wormsley, D. P., & D'Andrea, F. M. (Eds.). (1997). *Instructional strategies for Braille literacy.* New York: AFB Press.

Yopp, H. K. (1992). Developing phonemic awareness in young children. *Reading Teacher, 45*(9), 696–703.

Resources

This section provides just a sampling of the companies and organizations that can offer additional information, products, and services that will help teachers of braille reading and writing who are implementing the functional braille literacy program described in this book, as well as their students or clients. A more comprehensive listing of organizations and services can be found in the *AFB Directory of Services for Blind and Visually Impaired Persons,* published by the American Foundation for the Blind, which can also be searched electronically at the AFB web site, www.afb.org.

National Organizations

The following sample of national organizations in the field of visual impairment includes sources of assistance with literacy instruction in braille and links to other organizations, as well as additional information about and referrals to services for people who are blind or visually impaired.

AMERICAN COUNCIL OF THE BLIND
1155 15th Street N.W., Suite 1004
Washington, DC 20005
202-467-5081; 800-424-8666
Fax: 202-467-5085
www.acb.org
info@acb.org

A national consumer organization that serves as national clearinghouse for information and promotes the effective participation of blind people in all aspects of society. Provides information and referral; legal assistance and representation; scholarships; leadership and legislative training; consumer advocate support; assistance in technological research; a speaker referral service; consultative and advisory services to individuals, organizations, and agencies; and assistance with developing programs.

AMERICAN FOUNDATION FOR THE BLIND
11 Penn Plaza, Suite 300
New York, NY 10001
212-502-7600; 800-232-5463; 212-502-7662 (TDD/TTY); 800-232-3044 (book orders only)
Fax: 212-502-7777
www.afb.org
afbinfo@afb.net

An information clearinghouse for people who are blind or visually impaired and their families, professionals, organizations, schools, and corporations. Maintains the National Literacy Center in Atlanta, which develops resources on braille, assistive technology, and low vision, and provides up-to-date materials and training workshops for professionals. Also mounts program initiatives to improve services to visually impaired persons in aging, education, employment, and technology; conducts research and advocates for services and legislation; maintains the M.C. Migel Library and Information Center and the Helen Keller Archives; provides information and referral services; produces videos and publishes books, pamphlets, the *Directory of Services for Blind and Visually Impaired Persons in the United States and Canada*, the *Journal of Visual Impairment & Blindness*, and *AccessWorld: Technology and People with Visual Impairments*. Maintains offices around the country in Atlanta; Dallas; Huntington, WV; San Francisco; and Washington, D.C. In addition, AFB maintains the award-winning Braille Bug Web site (www.afb.org/braillebug) to promote braille literacy and provide public education about braille.

AMERICAN PRINTING HOUSE FOR THE BLIND

1839 Frankfort Avenue
Louisville, KY 40206-0085
502-895-2405; 800-223-1839
Fax: 502-899-2274
www.aph.org
info@aph.org

The official supplier of textbooks and educational aids for visually impaired students under federal appropriations. Promotes the independence of blind and visually impaired persons by providing specialized materials, products, and services needed for education and life. (See listing under Sources of Materials and Teaching Aids.)

ASSOCIATION FOR EDUCATION AND REHABILITATION OF THE BLIND AND VISUALLY IMPAIRED

1703 N. Beauregard Street, Suite 440
Alexandria, VA 22311
703-671-4500
Fax: 703-671-6391
www.aerbvi.org/
aer@aerbvi.org

A membership organization for professionals who work in all phases of education and rehabilitation with visually impaired persons of all ages on the local, regional, national, and international levels. Seeks to develop and promote professional excellence through such support services as continuing education, publications, information dissemination, lobbying and advocacy, and conferences and workshops. Publishes *RE:view*, a quarterly journal for professionals working in the field of blindness, and the newsletter *AER Report* and disseminates brochures and videotapes.

CALIFORNIA TRANSCRIBERS AND EDUCATORS OF THE VISUALLY HANDICAPPED

741 North Vermont Avenue
Los Angeles, CA 90029-3594
323-666-2211
www.ctevh.org

A membership organization for braille transcribers, educators and counselors in the field of visual impairment, family members, students, and others concerned with the special needs of individuals with visual impairment. Promotes acceptable practices and technology to enhance the total educational program for students who are visually impaired. Conducts workshops on braille code, transcribing techniques, and technology; publishes a basic guide to resources and *The CTEVH Journal;* and conducts an annual conference

COUNCIL FOR EXCEPTIONAL CHILDREN
Division on Visual Impairments
1110 North Glebe Road, Suite 300
Arlington, VA 22201-5704
703-620-3660; 888-CEC-SPED;
866-915-5000 (TTY, text only)
Fax: 703-264-9494
www.cec.sped.org
service@cec.sped.org
www.ed.arizona.edu/dvi/welcome.htm
(Division on Visual Impairments)

A professional organization for teachers, school administrators, practitioners, and others serving infants, children, and youths who require special services. Publishes periodicals, books, and other materials on teaching exceptional children; advocates for appropriate government policies; provides professional development; disseminates information on effective instructional strategies; and holds an annual conference. The Division on Visual Impairments focuses on the education of children who are visually impaired and the concerns of professionals who work with them and publishes the *DVI Quarterly* and has a stand in the annual national CEC conference.

HADLEY SCHOOL FOR THE BLIND
700 Elm Street
Winnetka, IL 60093-0299
847-446-8111; 800-323-4238
Fax: 847-446-9916
www.hadley-school.org/Web_Site/Hadley-School.asp

An accredited home-study school that provides tuition-free distance education courses for indi-
viduals who are visually impaired, family members, and professionals. Offers academic subjects, continuing education, family education, and professional education, including braille and other communication skills, independent living, technology, advocacy, and adjustment to blindness.

NATIONAL FEDERATION OF THE BLIND
1800 Johnson Street
Baltimore, MD 21230
410-659-9314
Fax: 410-685-5653
www.nfb.org
nfb@nfb.org

A national consumer organization, working to improve social and economic conditions of blind persons; monitors legislation affecting blind people; assists in promoting needed services; provides evaluation of present programs and assistance in establishing new ones; grants scholarships to blind persons; and conducts a public education program. Publishes the *Braille Monitor* and *Future Reflections*.

NATIONAL LIBRARY SERVICE FOR THE BLIND AND PHYSICALLY HANDICAPPED
Library of Congress
1291 Taylor Street, N.W.
Washington, DC 20542
202-707-5100; 800-424-8567;
202-707-0744 (TDD/TTY)
Fax: 202-707-0712
www.loc.gov/nls

A national program to distribute free reading materials in braille, on recorded disks and cassettes, or in Web-Braille to persons who are visually impaired and physically disabled who cannot utilize ordinary printed materials.

TEXAS SCHOOL FOR THE BLIND AND VISUALLY IMPAIRED

1100 West 45th Street
Austin, TX 78756
512-454-8631; 512-206-9451 (TDD)
Fax: 512-206-9450
www.tsbvi.edu

The web site of the Texas School for the Blind and Visually Impaired offers a large variety of resources for professionals, parents, and lay persons associated with programs for the visually impaired and deaf/blind throughout the state, country, and world. The section on braille includes a variety of resources, including downloadable files of braille books for different ages and other; lists of transcribers; fact sheets; and other resources for teachers and parents.

Specialized Curricula for Teaching Braille Reading and Writing

Most curriculum materials for teaching reading and writing were designed for print readers and therefore do not provide for any consistent introduction of braille contractions. The curriculum materials listed here, however, were designed with braille specifically in mind and are currently available from the organizations indicated. Contact information for these organizations follows the lists of curricula.

Braille Reading Curricula

BRAILLE CONNECTION: A BRAILLE READING AND WRITING PROGRAM FOR FORMER PRINT READERS, by H. Caton, B. Gordon, E. Pester, C. Roderick, and B. Modaressi
Designed for adventitiously blinded adults. Available from American Printing House for the Blind

BRAILLE FUNDAMENTALS, by J. Cleveland, N. Levack, D. Sewell, and R. Toy
Deisgned for primary to high school students. Available from Texas School for the Blind and Visually Impaired

BRAILLE TOO, by N. Hepker and S. C. Coquillette
Designed for older junior or senior high school students. The organization of the materials initally parallels the introduction of letters in the *Mangold Developmental Program of Tactile Perception and Braille Letter Recognition*. Available from Grant Wood Area Education Agency

MANGOLD DEVELOPMENTAL PROGRAM OF TACTILE PERCEPTION AND BRAILLE LETTER RECOGNITION, by S. S. Mangold
Provides for a systematic development of tracking patterns and hand movements. Also introduces all the letters of the alphabet in braille. Can be used with children and adults. Available from Exceptional Teaching Aids

PATTERNS: THE PRIMARY BRAILLE
READING PROGRAM, by H. Caton,
E. Pester, and E. J. Bradley
Designed for elementary age children. Available from American Printing House for the Blind

Braille Writing Curricula

BRAILLEWRITING DOT BY DOT
Teaches writing using the Perkins brailler and the slate and stylus. Works with a wide age range of individuals. Available from American Printing House for the Blind

LITERARY BRAILLE
PRACTICE SENTENCES
Reinforces the rules of the code in writing. Sentences are useful in dictation, especially with older students who have been using braille in reading but who may need more work on writing. Available from Exceptional Teaching Aids

TEACHING THE BRAILLE SLATE
AND STYLUS, by P. Mangold
Provides tips and techniques for teaching writing with the slate and stylus. Useful with students of any age. Available from Exceptional Teaching Aids

THE SLATE BOOK: A GUIDE
TO THE SLATE AND STYLUS, by J. Dunnam
Presents information about how to use the slate and stylus and provides practice sentences. Available from National Federation of the Blind

Sources of Curricula

AMERICAN PRINTING HOUSE
FOR THE BLIND
1839 Frankfort Avenue
Louisville, KY 40206-0085
502-895-2405; 800-223-1839
Fax: 502-899-2274
www.aph.org
info@aph.org

EXCEPTIONAL TEACHING AIDS
20102 Woodbine Avenue
Castro Valley, CA 94546
510-582-4859; 800-549-6999
Fax: 510-582-5911
www.exceptionalteaching.com/

GRANT WOOD AREA
EDUCATION AGENCY
4401 Sixth Street, S.W.
Cedar Rapids, IA 52404-4499
391-399-6700; 800-332-8488;
319-399-6766 (TDD)
Fax: 319-399-6457
www.aea10.k12.ia.us

NATIONAL FEDERATION
FOR THE BLIND
National Center for the Blind
Materials Center
1800 Johnson Street
Baltimore, MD 21230
410-659-9314
www.kifwebe.com/asp/default.asp

**TEXAS SCHOOL FOR THE BLIND
AND VISUALLY IMPAIRED**
1100 West 45th Street
Austin, TX 78756
512-454-8631; 512-206-9451 (TDD)
Fax: 512-206-9450
www.tsbvi.edu

Sources of Materials and Teaching Aids

This section lists some of the sources for the materials and teaching aids mentioned in this book as well as other products that can be useful in carrying out a braille literacy program.

**AMERICAN PRINTING HOUSE
FOR THE BLIND**
1839 Frankfort Avenue
Louisville, KY 40206-0085
502-895-2405; 800-223-1839
Fax: 502-899-2274
www.aph.org

Manufactures and distributes a wide assortment of educational and daily living products including the Swing Cell, slates and styli, Perkins Brailler, Swail Dot Inverter, Peg slate, Big Cell, braille calendars, braille paper. Publishes braille, large-print, recorded, CD-ROM, and tactile graphic publications; print-braille books, manufactures a wide assortment of educational and daily living products; modifies and develops computer-access equipment and software; maintains an educational research and development program concerned with educational methods and educational aids; and provides a reference-catalog service for volunteer-produced textbooks in all media for students who are visually impaired and for information about other sources of related materials.

CRESTWOOD COMMUNICATION AIDS
6625 N. Sidney Place
Milwaukee, WI 53209-3259
414-352-5678
Fax: 414-352-5679
www.communicationaids.com/

Distributes talking card readers as well as a variety of adapted communication devices.

EXCEPTIONAL TEACHING AIDS
20102 Woodbine Aveue
Castro Valley, CA 94546
510-582-4859; 800-549-6999
Fax: 510-582-5911
www.exceptionalteaching.com/

Manufactures and distributes a wide variety of educational materials and curricula, especially for children with special needs, including tactile marking dots, Wikki Stix, shelf liner to use in place of Dycem, and rubber mats for braillers.

FLAGHOUSE
601 Flaghouse Drive
Hasbrouck Heights, NJ 07604-3116
800-221-5185; 800-793-7900
www.flaghouse.com
info@flaghouse.com

Sells a variety of products, including Dycem nonslip material.

**HOWE PRESS OF PERKINS SCHOOL
FOR THE BLIND**
175 North Beacon Street
Watertown, MA 02472
617-926-3490
Fax: 617-926-2027
www.perkins.pvt.k12.ma.us/area.php?id=9

Manufactures and distributes the Perkins braillers, including one-handed and other versions, slates and styli, and braille paper and extended keys for one-handed brailling.

PCI EDUCATIONAL PUBLISHING
P.O. Box 34270
San Antonio, TX 78265-4270
800-594-4263
Fax: 888-259-8284
www.pcicatalog.com/

Distributes a variety of educational products, including talking card readers.

QUANTUM TECHNOLOGY PTY LTD
5 South Street
P.O. Box 390
Rydalmere NSW 2116
Australia
+61 2 8844 9888)
Fax: +61 2 9684 4717
www.quantech.com.au/index.html

Manufactures the Mountabatten Brailler.

Sources of Assessments

This section lists the sources of several assessment tools that are discussed in the text.

**DYNAMIC INDICATORS OF BASIC EARLY
LITERACY SKILLS (DIBELS)**
dibels.uoregon.edu/

TEXAS PRIMARY READING INVENTORY
Texas Education Agency
1701 North Congress Ave
Austin, TX 78701-1494
512-463-9734
www.tpri.org/

LEARNING MEDIA ASSESSMENT
Texas School for the Blind and Visually
Impaired
1100 West 45th Street
Austin, TX 78756-3494
512-454-8631
Fax: 512-206-9450
www.tsbvi.edu

**ASSESSMENT OF BRAILLE
LITERACY SKILLS**
Region IV Education Service Center
7145 West Tidwell
Houston, TX 77092-2096
713-462-7708
Fax: 713-744-8148
www.esc4.net

Sources of Braille Books and Reading Materials

There are many producers of braille books and related materials, including print-braille books, a few of which are listed here. Most of them provide catalogs of the books and reading materials that are available in braille.

Readers interested in determining if a particular book exists in braille may wish to consult the Louis Database of Accessible Materials for People Who Are Blind or Visually Impaired maintained by the American Printing House for the Blind. The Louis Database contains information about tens of thousands of titles of accessible materials, including braille, large print, sound recordings, and computer files from over 170 agencies throughout the United States. Louis can be accessed on the Internet at www.aph.org or by telephone at 800-223-1839.

**AMERICAN PRINTING HOUSE
FOR THE BLIND**
1839 Frankfort Avenue
Louisville, KY 40206-0085
502-895-2405; 800-223-1839
Fax: 502-899-2274
www.aph.org

BRAILLE INSTITUTE OF AMERICA
741 North Vermont Avenue
Los Angeles, CA 90029-3594
Fax: 213-663-0867
www.brailleinstitute.org

BRAILLE INTERNATIONAL
The William A. Thomas Braille Bookstore
3290 S.E. Slater Street
Stuart, FL 34997
561-286-8366; 800-336-3142
Fax: 561-286-8909
www.brailleintl.org/wat.htm

NATIONAL BRAILLE PRESS
88 St. Stephen Street
Boston, MA 02115
617-266-6160; 888-965-8965 (toll-free)
Fax: 617-437-0456
www.nbp.org/index.html

**NATIONAL LIBRARY SERVICE
FOR THE BLIND AND PHYSICALLY
HANDICAPPED**
Library of Congress
1291 Taylor Street, N.W.
Washington, DC 20542
202-707-5100; 800-424-8567
Fax: 202-707-0712
www.loc.gov/nls

**SEEDLINGS: BRAILLE BOOKS
FOR CHILDREN**
P.O. Box 51924
Livonia, MI 48151-5924
734-427-8552; 800-777-8552
www.seedlings.org

Sources of High-Interest, Low-Vocabulary Books

The high-interest, low-vocabulary books produced by the companies listed here are available in print, with the exception of those from the American Printing House for the Blind, which are available in large print or braille. Readers may want to search for books on topics that they know are of interest to their specific students, and then search the Louis database maintained by APH or the catalogs of the braille publishers listed in the previous section to see if these books are already available in braille. If books are not already available in braille, it is possible to have them brailled by one of the various transcriber organizations, which can be located through the National Library Service (see the section on National Organizations), or the *AFB Directory of Services.*

ACADEMIC COMMUNICATION ASSOCIATES
Publication Center, Dept. 611
4149 Avenida de la Plata
P.O. Box 4279
Oceanside, CA 92052-4279
760-758-9593; 888-758-9558
Fax: 760-758-1604
www.acadcom.com/

AMERICAN PRINTING HOUSE FOR THE BLIND
1839 Frankfort Avenue
Louisville, KY 40206-0085
502-895-2405; 800-223-1839
Fax: 502-899-2274
www.aph.org

CAPSTONE PRESS
151 Good Counsel Drive
P.O. Box 669
Mankato, MN 56002-0669
800-747-4992
Fax: 888-262-0705
www.capstone-press.com/

GLOBE FEARON EDUCATIONAL PUBLISHER
Pearson Learning Group
135 South Mount Zion Road
P.O. Box 2500
Lebanon, IN 46052
800-526-9907
Fax: 800-393-3156
www.globefearon.com/contact.cfm

ACADEMIC THERAPY PUBLICATIONS
20 Commercial Boulevard
Novato, CA 94949
800-422-7249
Fax: 888-287-9975
www.academictherapy.com/support/about
hnb.tpl?cart=1060560500650501

LAKESHORE LEARNING MATERIALS
2695 E. Dominguez Street
P.O. Box 6261
Carson, CA 90749
800-421-5354
Fax: 310-537-5403
www.lakeshorelearning.com

THE LERNER PUBLISHING GROUP
1251 Washington Avenue North
Minneapolis, MN 55401
800-328-4929
Fax: 800-332-1132
www.lernerbooks.com

NEW READERS PRESS
P.O. Box 35888
Syracuse, NY 13235-5888

800-448-8878
Fax: 866-894-2100
www.laubach.org/NRP/NewReadersPress.html

PERFECTION LEARNING CORPORATION
1000 North Second Avenue
P.O. Box 500
Logan, IA 51546-0500
800-831-4190
Fax: 800-543-2745
www.plconline.com

SADDLEBACK EDUCATIONAL, INC.
3 Watson
Irvine, CA 92618
888-735-2225
Fax: 888-734-4010
www.sdlback.com

STECK VAUGHN
Box 26015
Austin, TX 78755
800-531-5015
Fax: 800-699-9459
www.steckvaughn.com/

Index

About the Author

Diane P. Wormsley, Ph.D, is Program Director of the Professional Preparation Program in Education of Children with Visual and Multiple Disabilities at the Pennsylvania College of Optometry in Philadelphia. She was previously Education Manager at the Overbrook School for the Blind in Philadelphia and Director of the American Foundation for the Blind's National Initiative on Literacy. Dr. Wormsley is co-author of *Instructional Strategies for Braille Literacy* (winner of the 1997 award for best title in Nursing/Allied Health from the Association of American Publishers Professional and Scholarly Publishing Division and of the C. Warren Bledsoe Award from the Association for Education and Rehabilitation of the Blind and Visually Impaired), *Braille Literacy Curriculum,* and *Foundations of Braille Literacy* and the companion video, *Understanding Braille Literacy.* In addition, she has authored many articles, book chapters, and presentations on braille, braille literacy, and braille education. A certified teacher of students who are visually impaired and hearing impaired, she has taught children in New York State, Pennsylvania, Australia, and Papua New Guinea.